"PINCH" OF SICILY

"PINCH" OF SICILY

✦

A COLLECTION OF MEMORIES AND TRADITIONAL RECIPES

Maria Sciortino

iUniverse, Inc.
New York Lincoln Shanghai

"PINCH" OF SICILY
A COLLECTION OF MEMORIES AND TRADITIONAL RECIPES

iUniverse books may be ordered through booksellers or by contacting:

iUniverse
2021 Pine Lake Road, Suite 100
Lincoln, NE 68512
www.iuniverse.com
1-800-Authors (1-800-288-4677)

ISBN-13: 978-0-595-37552-3 (pbk)
ISBN-13: 978-0-595-81946-1 (ebk)
ISBN-10: 0-595-37552-9 (pbk)
ISBN-10: 0-595-81946-X (ebk)

Printed in the United States of America

Dedicated to Bianca, Vincent, Alexandra, Gianna, Sophia and Isabella

My children have heard these stories repeated so many times that they must be bored with them. As your grandmother, I want you to become acquainted with your origins.

Since you are all very young, I am unable to speak to you of your heritage. I have hoped one day, with the help of God, to share my legacy with all my grandchildren. As you mature, I pray that you understand me with gratitude and appreciation.

Contents

Acknowledgements

I am grateful to my son's and my grand children, they are the reason why I chose to write this memoir. Special thanks to my parents, who sent me too school. I have the ability to write. I am grateful to my brother and my sister, who gave to me the correct proportion for the recipe.

Special thanks to the *bravo giornalista* Stepano Vaccara who was the first person to encourage me into publishing my long trip to America. Addition thanks go to Kevin Cascone who helped me with my English writing, correcting me and helping me through the way. As I helped him with the Italian Language, today he is President in the Italian club in his school. Thanks to Ariana, Daniela, Laureen, Fran, and Guiseppe Verde for their true understanding for what I really wanted to say.

I am grateful that everyone gives me the support to write, like Elena with her Italian American culture, which helped me transfer my thoughts. I am grateful to Geraldine and Paul Rue that has helped me with additional information. Thanks to all those I have failed to mention those who helped and inspired me.

And finally I am most grateful to my husband—without his help, I would have never been able to finish this memoir. He would go to sleep alone because I would be up writing so many nights; because it was then I had time to remember and concentrate to write.

Maria–Sciortino

Introduction

Any communications, observations and comments should be addressed to the Author,
sicilianpinch@yahoo.com

Preface

WHY AM I WRITING THIS BOOK?

I love to communicate, especially through writing. I often feel the necessity to write. I love to put all of my feelings on paper and to write about my homeland and America, which for me was a new and different culture.

I became serious about creating a diary and putting my family story together soon after the birth of my grandchildren, Bianca and Vincent. Their births were what gave me the motivation to write. I wanted to leave them an inheritance (not a financial one, I am not rich), but a record of culture to remind my Sciortinellis (the affectionate name we give to the young Sciortinos) who we are and where we came from. When I started to write my stories, there were only two grandchildren. Today God has blessed me with six grandchildren. So now I have to sit and write and try to remember. I hope one day some of them can identify with this material in some way to say, "I am happy and proud to be a part of this family that came to America to build their own "nest." I hope they come to know their grandparents supported their family with hard, honest work, leaving this inheritance as well as the Sciortino name to their grandchildren.

We came to America, maybe not just out of necessity, but more a vague dream to explore a modern world on the other side, to see what it could offer us—to transform our young lives for the better. We ran blind to a new land, where we did not know the language or the culture. We looked for chances to learn, to follow, to change and soon, hopefully, to become one of them. Internally we fought with ourselves to remain who we were. We did not want to lose our culture, and more importantly, our identity. We wanted to keep our culture intact so that we could leave it to our descendants.

I have had the idea of writing this book for a long time. What sparked the inspiration to write was my reading the book entitled, "The Italian Americans"? I saw part of my life and thought of writing my memories.

1

1.1. MEMORIES OF SICILY

I write these memories not only for my grandchildren, but out of nostalgia for my native land. I have a deep love for my home town in Sicily, the land of my birth. The fishing town is situated on a hill, descending with a gentle downward slope, to the Mediterranean Sea. So many different people invaded this beautiful island of Sicily and they came through my town, which was once called by the Arabic name Xacca. It is called Sciacca now, but it is also known as "Sciacca Terme" for its healthy water and sulfur mud. It is one of the oldest and best thermal resorts in Sicily. Visited by Princess Salina from Giuseppe Tomasso's story Il Gattopardo, today it is a most modern, sophisticated, and well equipped spa.

We have so many traditions, superstitions and folktale that I will tell about. Sciacca is a city of "Sun & Sea". It produces fresh sea food, hot fragrant bread, and outstanding wines, which are made from rich ripe grapes on our fertile ground. When I close my eyes I can see Sciacca like a beautiful water color picture, with little red roof houses, overlooking sandy beaches. The balconies are full of pots with beautiful smelling white *gelsomini* (jasmine) and colorful *gerani* (geraniums), which bloom all year round.

There are very little twisty narrow streets, and people greet other people from one balcony to the next. They say "Good Morning". There are little court yards everywhere that look like labyrinths. Walking up from the sea towards town, you soon reach Piazza Scandaliato (*lu Chianu*). It is a couple of hundred meters of rectangular piazza, like a balcony of red coral topping the town. The soft happy aromas feel somehow like the beach sand. In the summer time, you sit in the famous bar terrace overlooking the sea to sip a good *espresso* coffee or a delicious tasting cold gelato. You would admire the view of all the boat on the port that were full of fresh fish when they come back from a hard day of fishing

Our piazza in Sciacca is like a family living room for various kinds of happenings *riunioni, discorsi, incontri amorosi, pettegolezzi*-meetings of all kinds, discussions and speeches, amorous encounters, gossiping. When I was a teenager our strict parents said we could not go to the piazza, not even to take a walk. We wanted especially to show off our newly styled outfits and to maybe meet a boyfriend. We took the chance to go off to take a walk there, up and down, for many hours. Maybe to smile at each other and to give a silent message (it was pro-hibited to have any contact before the engagement). We would sneak away from our mothers, who were relaxing under the big trees full of oxygen that brought coolness and relief from the summer heat. I remember the beautiful silk fans with decorated *ventagli* they carried if they thought that it was not cool enough. If we would walk a little fur-ther we would be in front of a beautiful Art Deco villa with manicured flowers and statues, which is the magnificent view you get of the famous Sciacca Terme Spa along the sea.

Still walking uphill in my hometown, you find yourself in a food market in a shopping piazza. Every morning the farmers bring their crops, and you will find all kinds of herbs and fresh aromas there. Everyday looks like a holiday, with people shopping and looking for the best quality at the cheapest price. Continuing uphill by walking up the steep stairs, you are at San Michele church. Nearby there is the big round piazza Gerardo Noceto, where every Saturday they had a large outdoor market. So many venders come from other places other than Sicily, bringing their own merchandise, and not only fresh foods like some roasted chicken with a side of fried potatoes, but clothing and accessories too. All the merchandise is displayed by the sellers screaming about their quality at their low prices. Here you would need a half hour to negotiate, and might get the right price. The side walk sale is very interesting and crowded. If you are looking for someone, you would absolutely meet them here while shopping or gossiping.

Go through Porta San Calogero and you see the antique Castello Luna, an old fort home of one of the most powerful and rich medieval families that owned land in this area. The Luna family had a huge feud with another rich and powerful family, the Perollos, whom they had been fighting for more two hundred years. Turn your head up and you see the farmers working the land opposite. The odor is of dry fertile ground, and as you admire the yellow *ginestra* (broom), you realize they are part of their own unique Mediterranean odor. Now look up to see the beautiful mountain of *San Calogero*, containing an ancient complex of underground water-eroded caverns, rich in tales of archaeology as well as history. The caves are full of hot sulfurous vapors known to be good for the health. Admire the monastery with its ancient ceramics and amazing statue of Saint Calogero, the town protector, standing out over the city. I think of Sciacca and I think this always: "Sciacca is a small city with a big heart".

1.2. A PINCH (*UN PIZZICO*)

What is a pinch? It is a very, very small portion of something. So small that it can fit between your thumb and index fingers.

A pinch is something essential for completeness in food—just enough to give it the right taste.

A pinch is used to better express our feelings—to help someone understand what we cannot say in words—so we use our hands. Sicilians are famous for this!

The Sicilians are made from a pinch of their ancestors—ancient tribes, Romans, Arabs, Greeks, Spanish. Each of them gave us a pinch of their own culture, kindness, madness, wisdom, stupidity and thanks to some of them, the will to survive—and that final pinch of good luck.

Years ago we valued our food—making sure that portions were adequate. We did not have scales to measure the amount of food—we did it with the palm of our hands. But things like salt and pepper were very expensive and hard to get. We rubbed it between our thumb and index fingers so there would be just enough for the perfect taste.

My mother, with her soft voice and modest manner, always cautioned me "N*on strafare* (never overdo it)." She would say—it is not an abundance of ingredients that makes the food good but it is just "that pinch of salt" that gives the *minestra* (soup) the perfect taste.

As an infant, your mother caressed you with a soft *pizzicotto* (a soft pinch on the cheek) to reassure you that she was there to protect you.

A teenage boy might take a chance to pass near a young girl to take advantage of an opportunity to give her a pinch so that maybe she would understand that he liked her.

You husband, perhaps after a long hard day of work, would return home, kiss you, caress you and with a little pinch on your backside—without any words—would tell you that he wanted to make love to you.

And when you grow older, when you think that passion has vanished and when you are sure that nothing works anymore—it is not really that way. The hand—it still moves, it can stretch and it is ready for that touch. Take the thumb and index/pointer and rub them together—like a caress—that final pinch of spice—necessary to complete the taste of a "good dish of life". That passionate pinch—tells it all—"I am still here—I love you".

1.3. THE STORY BEGINS

I was born and raised in Sciacca, in Sicily. My childhood was normal, full of family and friends, because my family cared. My parents tried to do their best even during financially difficult times. They didn't want any of the children to feel the "pinch" of want. Our closeness helped us to face and overcome all our problems and obstacles. We were able to appreciate what we had.

Our days passed happily. Women stayed home doing chores and listening to the radio. We adored listening to the love songs by the orchestra Angelini. We enjoyed Nilla Pizzi, who was a popular singer. I cherished reading magazines and books. Many times instead of doing the job of dusting my brothers' bookcase I would read for hours.

In 1956 our TV arrived in our home (not everyone was able to have one then). Before that on Saturdays we would get together at our neighbor's place and each person would bring his or her own chair. We watched programs such as *il Musichiere* with Mario Riva or *il Festival di San Remo*. In those days, there was only one channel. Naturally, each viewer was forced to watch the same program. They had a program called *Carosello* where a few companies got together and presented their merchandise, like a show. The beginnings of QVC!

Women copied hairstyles and wore dresses like actresses or singers appeared in on T.V. shows. People already had started to talk about America, because we saw movies with Rita Hayworth and Lana Turner. The US show with Perry Como was my favorite.

My small seaside city was divided into three geographical parts: the sea, the plains, and the countryside. Even working (non-professional) people were divided into three categories: sailors, artisans and farmers. They married people within their category. But as time went on and the town became more urbanized, people were able to marry anybody.

My family owned some land. The head man in the family had the title of Don. My grandfather was Don Pasquale. He had some land and men who worked for him. My grandfather wanted something different for my father. My dad was able to study and start a business. Things went well for a while. After the war the situation changed for the worse. In fact, the land lost its value.

The young people did not want to be in agriculture, they wanted to emigrate. My father did too. He received a visa and with enthusiasm he flew to America. On the other side, in the fifties, the first American tourists arrived in Sicily with their big cars (but were unable to drive on our small streets!). This was the first time I saw chewing gum. I was a child when the Americans freed Sicily and I knew America from TV and movies.

In the late Fifties, I had my first boyfriend who was only able to say hello to me, and sometimes I would talk to him secretly. It was not permitted for young people to have a casual relationship. You had to be seriously involved to have any contact. I would say I was going out with a girlfriend and actually saw him, and we got engaged on August 12th, 1959. And America was all he talked about.

1.4. ONE YEAR OF SICILIAN TRADITIONS

Here are my memories of the important events and feasts that are particular to each month of the year

1.4.1. January: New Year's Day

Sciacca has many important holidays and events like all Italian cities regardless of the city's size. Because of the different categories of people (farmers, fishermen, artisans, and doctors), each family celebrated the same holiday with different family and food traditions. Each month had its own important feast; sometimes there was more than one. There was usually an important religious holiday every month.

My family celebrated *la notte di San Silvestro,* also called *Capodanno,* the night of New Years. It was always a special family reunion with my grandparents. We had a late dinner usually at 12:00 AM. My mother fried the fresh sausages with black olives and virgin olive oil for a dish called *passuluna.* The aroma was so good it suggested good things to come and as we used to say, it "makes the stomach ready." In the meantime we cut half a lemon, squeezed the juice on top of the sausages and dipped the bread in that exquisite dressing.

We toast to the New Year with *spumante,* sparkling wine. An *espresso* coffee follows with a piece of *panettone,* raised Italian holiday cake. After we finish we looked for something old: dishes, pots or something that would make a lot of noise. For we threw them from the balcony, throwing the old and bad things away in hopes the New Year will bring something new and good. *Buon Anno Buona Fortuna* Happy New Year and good fortune, too.

The first day of the New Year we went to church and took a walk in the piazza (to show off the new coat we received), to greet and speak with our relatives and friends and to wish them a Happy New Year.

Then we walked back home to help my mother and grandmother, who were already working in the kitchen preparing the celebratory meals. I put on a festive apron ready to sauté with my sister.

Almost every year we made *arancine,* filled Sicilian rice balls (see recipes section). My sister was especially good at rolling them in the eggs and breadcrumbs. They are deep fried in oil in a regular old frying pan (we never had an electric frying pan). My job was to set the dining room table but in the meantime while setting the table I would sneak some of the food into my mouth, making sure no one saw. I love to taste of this special food, especially the hot tomato sauce. While it is boiling it is very tempting to dip in a piece of bread and enjoy…what a taste!!

We started dinner each time with pasta and *ragù* sauce (tomato, meat, vegetables like peas), then one or two meatballs and two pieces of potatoes. Yes potatoes, because we made our *ragù* sauces with a couple of potatoes cut in pieces. This was because first, it tastes very good in the sauce, and second because it helps to fill the dishes (it is too expensive to make meatballs with only meat) instead of all that meat. Then each person would get one piece of veal and salad.

Next my mother put on the little Neapolitan coffee pot, filling one sector with water and the other with ground coffee and closed it tight. When the water boiled she would turn the pot upside down and the hot water passed easily to the side containing the ground coffee. The coffee would go down a long funnel from the pot and a little puff of steam would come out. The aroma gave an indescribable odor, and you would start to taste the irreplaceable drink. You never wanted to miss it, accompanied by the sweet *pignulata* (see recipes), little pieces of sweet egg dough, fried and in oil and caramelized with honey). Sometimes we had fruit, and sometimes not, until we were satisfied.

My sister and I would then get up and start to clean the table. She washed the dishes and I dried. We seldom had leftovers. Everything was rationed equally; nothing was wasted or refrigerated, because we did not have a refrigerator. If we had something leftover we would eat it in the night, or put it in a dish and leave it on the balcony, ready for the next day. In the meantime my parents and grandparents talked and we were all happy at the end of the day to have such a nice holiday together.

1.4.2. February: *Carnevale*

This month is the coldest one in the year, as we say in Sicilian dialect, *fivàru cuttu e amaru* (February short and cold). At the end of the month is celebrated Fat Tuesday or Mardi Gras in French, but we Sicilians called it *Carnevale*. The week before the Thursday Carnival, the town got together every afternoon, like a big family, in the Piazza to celebrate with music, dance and to see the famous allegorical floats, which were then little more than carts. The people dressed in fantastical costumes and the themes of their costumes and of the floats were creatively geared toward making fun of famous politicians or scandalous happenings of that time. All the songs involved caricatures of these themes. Lots of people, dressed in antique costumes, were each day walking the city streets and stopping their friends to throw on them colorful *confetti* and to guess the identity of whom their costumes represented.

The proverb for that holiday was: *Carnevale: ogni scherzo vale* (in Carnival every joke is ok). So every person tried to have as good a time as possible, before the forty days of Lent began, and jokes and laughter could be heard everywhere. My father went to the piazza early in the morning to greet and gather with his friends and go to his favorite coffee shop called *Bartolino*.

The most famous traditional cart was *Peppi Nnappa*. It is still the best known and best loved cart in the Sciacca Carnavale, and always comes last. At the end of Carnavale, it is burned each year in a giant bonfire.

Every family enjoyed a very rich dinner, with pork roast and sausages. After dinner finished we had to decide which to serve first: coffee or fruit...such a dilemma! We served the dessert first, for we could not wait another minute for the delicious fresh Sicilian *cannoli*, pastry filled with *ricotta* (freshly sweet *pecorino* cheese) which was prepared fresh daily. They were sugared and carefully put on a carton tray, wrapped with paper and tied with colorful ribbons that had been curled. Ceremoniously my mother would open the tray and serve one to a person, which was for me the best moment of the holiday dinner. The men would sip the hot coffee...and a glass of good wine, and be happy and forget their troubles.

(This holiday was my fathers' favorite; he got married in this month—in February 1928. After 66 years of being married my father died one week before carnival time and two weeks after his 90th birthday (1904–1994). My mother died four years later at carnival time—February 10th–1909–1998).

My grandparents always made sure that we had this holiday together with my uncle and the family. In the afternoon my parents and I went to the piazza to see the fiesta. My grandparents never came to see the town party in the piazza. A few times some neighbors and friends invited us and a few more friends to organize a home dance, in those days even in small rooms. They would put the big records in the *grammofono* (record player). Sometimes they did not have enough chairs for everyone...No problem!!! *Le signorine* (girls) sat and *i Cavalieri* (gentlemen) stood up ready to invite their favorite girl for a dance. We had a good time dancing for what seemed like all night, but was really no later than 12 o'clock (with no food or drink, except maybe just a small glass of cordial).

A couple of times after my sister was a teenager we went to the *Veglione delle Terme*, (a special dance night in the Spa), organized by the *Circolo Unione* (men's club) to which my father belonged. Lots of the young people dressed in beautiful, colorful costumes or stylish evening gowns appropriate for the night. They were covered with *stelle filanti* (multicolored paper ribbons). The music and songs were plentiful for that special night. There were lots of waltzes, *tango* and *marzucca*.

The *marzucca* was an old dance that my father loved to dance with my mother, but she was too shy and embarrassed to dance. Instead, as soon as we girls grew up my father taught us to dance the *marzucca*. When we started to have boyfriends, we preferred to dance with them. My father would sit quietly and watch us, pretending he wanted to sit because he was tired (now that this time has passed, I feel badly, imagining my father and how he felt when his favorite song played.) At the end of the night a jury decided the best costume of the ball. One of my brother's girlfriends lent me a Persian costume for one night. I was really happy to wear it, even though I never won anything.

The day following the holiday was Ash Wednesday, when Catholic people went to church to receive ashes on their forehead. Others would prefer instead to go early in the morning to their farm in the countryside for a *scampagnata* (the day after) and start again with food, wine and many, many songs. Everyone sang their favorite songs or *stornelli*.

I want you to understand that we were not rich; we just had each other and a few things to bring our families together. We cooked a lot of pasta with sausages and egg frittata and a few homemade biscuits. With this small quantity of food we could have a good meal, with family and friends. Almost every family produced its own wine, from their own land and grapes. Each one brings a bottle and with our simple food we would feel as if we possessed the world.

1.4.3. March: Saint Joseph

Now in March there are only a few windy days as the temperature starts to rise and day by day it gets warmer. The holiday this month is on the 19th: St. Joseph's Day. It is important for us because it was the holiday in which we honored my humble mother named *Giuseppa* (feminine of Joseph, *Giuseppe*). She never asked for anything for herself. We tried to celebrate her onomastica, her name day, with her favorite simple dessert called li *sfingi* (funnel cake).

My sister prepared the soft dough and I helped by reading the recipe and running to the store to get the ingredients. After the dough matured and became very soft and elastic, she took a piece with a big spoon and dipped it in olive oil (we never used vegetable oil), and it is fried. Afterward she took baking paper and covered it with fine powdered sugar. We cut some in the middle and filled them with a soft Bavarian cream or sweet ricotta and they became sweet *bocconcino* (cream puff). This was the only way for us to show our dear mother our love. At this time there was not yet a recognized *giornata della Mamma* (Mothers Day).

The mother was the person who was ready to do everything at anytime for the family and never asked for anything in return. We never threw a party for her; we seldom had a party. We really never had a party for anyone in the family. For a big event we had an intimate dinner with the family. In Sicily years ago we only celebrated the *onomastico*, not birthdays. I never remember celebrating a birthday for my parents or my brothers and sister. We were taught to be peaceful and humble, and not to ask for many things. I had my first birthday celebration when I was 21. My boyfriend sent me a bouquet of roses and a birthday cake. What a present!! It was the first time I blew out candles. Now people all over the world celebrate birthdays the same way. After television came, everybody mirrored each other's style—throwing a party for every little occasion and being together with your family and dear friends.

But for my mother Giuseppa-Happy Mothers Day!!! You will remain in my heart forever.

1.4.4. April: *Buona Pasqua a tutti*—HAPPY EASTER TO EVERYONE

In April, for the beautiful Catholic feast of *Pasqua* (Easter), all the church bells in the town rang their festive chimes inviting all to go to church for the Easter Sunday Mass. The weather warmed up and it is finally springtime. The sun is now with us everyday. At last it is time to wear light clothing and take a walk in the piazza in the new fashions. After greeting our relatives we took a walk through the piazza to assist in the very touching *incontro* (meeting). It is a tradition in which statues from the churches are brought out into the piazza, with that of the archangel Gabriel, announcing to Mary that her son is alive, and of one of her son that is borne towards them until they meet.

Upon returning home, as I reach the top of the steps I start to smell the delicious aroma from the *capretto*, which is young lamb *ragù* my dear mother had already prepared. The kitchen door was near the entrance door, at the left side. I would report to my mother all the friends that wished her well and sent their greetings. When that aroma over stimulated my appetite again, I took advantage of my table setting duties and secretly tasted some of the prepared and covered food that was ready to be put on the table. I was happy to set the table with a special festive white linen tablecloth and napkins.

My preference for the Easter table would be for a colorful tablecloth with lots of flowers but the colored tablecloth was for the weekdays. The flowers on the Easter table were white lilies, the symbol of purity. My mother would open the *credenza* (China closet) and take out the *porcellana* (porcelain) Bavarian dishes, an old family wedding gift, used only for special holidays. After my mother's death we split them up with just a few dishes each. I also have the coffee pot and now they are in my credenza and I never use them because they are so precious and I don't want them to be accidentally broken.

The silverware we had was a regular daily set, the same as every day. Even the glasses were not an expensive crystal set, just regular glasses. The wine bottle was the same all the time too; it was filled for the meal from the *barile* (barrel). For water we used only a small glass. At that time, we only drink a very small amount because we had heard that water fills the stomach and spoils the appetite. Everyone preferred one half glass of wine to help with the digestion anyway. (How times change! Today we are told to drink at least 8 glasses of water a day.) Ice? forget about it!! We did not even have a refrigerator; as I already said, even cold water was prohibited then because it was said to be bad for the digestion.

At my father's arrival we would sit and say a blessing, and then start to eat the succulent dinner. First pasta, *capretto al forno* (young roasted lamb) seasoned with a lot of wild herbs and wine to give that delicious taste. Salad, then coffee and cake; the famous *cassata siciliana* (home-made sponge cake, filled with sweet layers of ricotta and citrus fruits (see recipe section).

1.4.5. May: MAYDAY, my *nonna*.

The first of May in Italy is a national holiday, *la festa del lavoro* (Labor Day). Nobody works on this day!!! From the early morning on everybody goes to the farm to bond with Mother Nature. The temperature is much warmer and the soil smells fresh, and for many it is the first chance to escape the busy city. I remember how I enjoyed breathing the healthy oxygen and seeing the trees full of green leaves. Our farm is only a few kilometers distant from the city. I would take a long pleasant walk into the garden which was like a paradise of agrumi (citrus) and *oliveti* (olive groves).

This is the most beautiful season for the farm; you can abandon reality for a dream, or just admire the lovely daisies covering the soil. I would be torn between whether to look at the sky or dig the rich soil with my hands, a feeling so natural and pleasant that only Mother Nature can offer it! In that moment the ground became like an antibiotic medicine, taking away the infection of your thoughts and clearing the brain. The farmers would already have been seeding and working with the hoes, and sometimes already watering from the well if there had not been enough rain. On this day we would look at nature's work; after humans put in so much work caring for their plants and with no work by humans for the wild plants, Nature still made them all blossom each year with flowers and fresh and natural fruits and vegetables.

The first vision of the farm was that one of *miei nonni* (my grandparents). My *nonna* (grandmother) would see us as we arrived and she would run to meet us with her arms wide open, happy to see us. She would cook for us fresh fried eggs from her chicken. She had a large hen house with chicks, roasters and turkeys. She would take the fresh bread she made every week and put it in her wood oven. The oven was heated by branches and sticks of olive trees and at the right temperature the tiles in the oven would turn red, and we would know the dough was ready to be baked, turning into most delicious bread.

She never possessed a thermometer or a gas stove, and she never had anything electrical or automatic. She never saw another country or another culture, and she never used cosmetics or perfume. She never had a shower or running water in her home. The only luxury she was permitted was a scented *saponetta* (face soap), with which she washed her face and body trying her best to do it with the water in one big bowl. However she was always clean and she was always well coordinated and dressed with elegance! I do not know what grade in school she completed but from the time that my grandfather was the provider of the family, she showed that she did not need a formal education! With her own good sense and instinct for well-being, plus a lot of intelligence, she was a treasured icon in our family. She was always so polite, and she was modern and opened up her heart to all of the family.

She married my grandfather at a very young age. The family usually looked for somebody of the same social class. My grandmother already had a nice man she was in love with but because he was in a different social situation she was not permitted to marry this man. My grandfather was a good and hard-working man, young too, and good looking, coming from a better family. To make a long story short, the engagement was made, and in a short time they were married (for love or no love, it was not important in those days).

He was a serious man and he did not have many friends but he was very hard working. He had a thing for work! He saved money and bought more property. His own personality was very much like Sicily: strong like the soul, cold and immense like the Mediterranean sea, looking shallow but so deep you could not see the bottom. He was educated by his rigorous father to be very careful not to talk too much or do anything wrong. That is, everything had to appear okay and nobody should know the affairs of the family. He barely showed any emotion of any kind; he seldom laughed and almost never touched, hugged or kissed us. He never demonstrated any tenderness to his wife. They conceived two sons by candlelight; maybe they never even saw each other's bodies. My grandmother never took off her socks in front of my grandfather; she would go to the other room, to make sure that nobody saw her naked leg. In that time "the stork brought the baby." Modesty was very important.

The wife was considered like *Stelluccia*, the wife in *Il Gattopardo*, or maybe more like the family dog; she was at all times at the ready to obey the master. But maybe the coldness and rigid feelings helped my grandmother to be a strong wife. She pretended to obey him all the time, but at the right moment she would know when to be a real *matriarca*, and with only one word she decided the entire family business. My grandmother was in love with her husband, and with time she discovered that inside the man's shell was hiding a really tender man, with an open heart. When he was alone with her he became a different man, only letting her know he did it for the *apparenza* (appearance). The man was supposed to look strong and serious!!!

She had an altogether different personality, happy and content with life. To us she was a teacher and a protector. She seemed the only person to really understand all life's problems and how to act to settle everything. She never worked on the farm. Her husband did not permit her to work outside of the house; she stayed home to cook, sew and crochet. She was a skinny woman with auburn hair, and I always remember her dressed either in a dark blue polka dot dress or in black to mourn the loss of a family member.

The dresses were straight and simple, tied with a belt at the waist; the sleeves were long even in the summertime. She would wear her hair in a big bun the time, tied with an elastic holder that she sewed herself. But in some ways she was a rebel, for she never wore the black *scialle* (scarf), a Sicilian Moslem-like tradition embraced by many generations. She loved to keep her head uncovered and free, and she was proud not to have her father or husband persuade her to do so. She would wear the *spolverino* (light coat) in a soft blue material called *marocchino* that was a plain straight cut with long sleeves and a shawl collar with two pockets. She would wear it on Sunday or special days. At that time they did not have dry cleaners so in order to clean a spot off them, she would take a small rag and dip it in *benzina* (gasoline), clean off the dirt and let the coat hang for a few hours in the fresh air.

I imagine now sometimes how happy she must have been that she had lived long enough to see electricity on her farm. Finally, she could see her beautiful face clearly in the mirror. In the summer, as soon as school was finished, I wanted to see her and stay on the farm for a week. We always had a truly wonderful time and did many things together. Every afternoon we would say the devotion *Ave Maria*, and the refrain which was answered, *Santa Maria*.

The daily rosary for my *nonna* was a moment of prayer and meditation and as soon as she sat down to say it, she remembered something that she did not do during the day and she would get up then and complete it (things like making sure the door was locked and that the dog was outside guarding the house, etc.) Before we finished reciting the rosary it was already dark, and my *nonna* would light the candle with a cotton wick dipped in oil.

I remember being little and scared. My mind would be confused with emotions and I would start to cry because the light would flicker and scare me with the images I would see in the shadows. I would sit with my grandmother and she would take my hand and reassure me not to be afraid. My grandmother would tell me all the good things she had planned we were going to be doing; her week was very organized.

Every day there was something different: Monday we did the laundry; soaking the clothes in water using *liscivia*, a grey powder that comes from almond shells after they are dried, you put them in a rag and soak in water, something like "Clorox" today. For soap she used *potassa* which is a green rock that is boiled with another chemical turning it to a soft green soap. You only needed a pinch of the strong chemical to clean the laundry, and sometimes your fingers would become chapped from a lot of use of this stuff.

Tuesday we would wash and rinse, and, if it was a nice day, hang the cleaned clothes in the fresh air on a long line tied between two trees. In a few hours they were dry, and in the afternoon she would start to press with her heavy iron full of carbon (coal), she would iron every piece of fabric even a towel.

Wednesday we would take a walk and go see the trees in her lovely but simple garden full of all kinds of herbs, oregano, basil, mint, bay leaves, salvia (her favorite) and many more. When we returned we would sit and talk or she would teach me to crochet on her porch. On the right side of the house they had *la Pinnata* which was a sloping square gazebo made of *canne* (bamboo), with *canali* (clay gutter) and terracotta tile. It was perfect for relaxing and staying cool on the hot summer days.

Thursday we would take another walk but this time to visit some neighbors and bring them something like nuts or food. If the people were not home, we would put a rock in front of the steps or we would turn the rug upside down for a sign that we stopped by (they didn't have phones so we had no other way of communicating with them). As soon as the neighbor would see that we had visited she would come to our home for a while to talk and have some fruit and nuts. These neighbors would ask me lots of questions when they wanted to be informed of something new going on in the city, or else they might ask me to buy something for them in the city that I could bring back when I would return.

Friday, early in the morning she would start to make the bread, gathering sticks and branches for the oven. First she would make the pizza, very simply with little ripened tomatoes, she would squash them by hand and she then would grate some cheese, a few pieces *alici* (anchovies), oregano and a lot of pure olive oil. It would be baked for only a short time. Next she used a long wooden spatula to put the dough in the oven, leaving a space between each piece. Soon she took the spatula and one by one removed the bread, the smell of the fresh baked bread filled the room with a marvelous aroma. My grandmother would take the bread and cut it in the middle, and then she added fresh grated cheese. If you wanted more flavors, you could add a few pieces of anchovies, a pinch of salt and pepper and a lot of virgin olive oil. Then you would have for your eating pleasure the most delicious bread, called *pani cunzatu*. For that day, it was the only item for our dinner. On the holidays she would sometimes make *biscotti di mandorle* (almond biscuits), her favorite!

Saturday finally arrived, and so she started to prepare what she is going to bring the next day. She would put the food in a napkin tied at the four corners. Fruits, vegetables were placed in a *panaru* (wicker basket). My *nonno* (grandfather) would start to groom the horses and bring them to the blacksmith to clean their iron shoes. He would prepare the leather saddle, and then he would leave the horses to come home to prepare what he would be wearing the next day, seeing to his corduroy suit, the *coppola*, a typical Sicilian beret, and shining his shoes.

Sunday morning as soon as the sun rose, my *nonno* would take the horse from the stable and put him ready to drive the *carrozzino* (wagon). My *nonna* would be ready with festive clothing, a special comb tied in her hair, her face radiant with happiness and the basket with the food already prepared in her hand. I remember her as well as she stood in front of the door with the basket, getting ready to put everything into the wagon in the bottom compartment.

They then would sit down next each other and my nonno would give the horse a strap to send him off trotting. In 20 minutes we would reach the city. First we stopped at my house to bring everybody *ben di dio* (blessings of God) and to leave some of the things off, and then we would continue down the street arriving at their own home. My uncles lived together upstairs and my *nonna* was *felice* (happy) that she could see her children and grandchildren. We would then go to church, go shopping and visiting, usually some *comare* (children's godmother). *Nonno* would go to the barbershop for a cut or shave and do some shopping.

At 1:00, we would all go back to have dinner. In the afternoon my family would go and visit them. My *nonno* would go into the kitchen and bring us back a handful of almonds and roasted chicken, to give us as a treat. My *nonna* took the carton tray and offered us her homemade *biscotti*. As soon as our grandfather turned his face, my grandmother gave us some change to buy some candies. She hid this from him because he thought she was spoiling us and did not agree with spoiling us with treats.

Some Sundays for any very special occasion they remained in the city and slept in our house. For all of us it was a big treat. During the night, I asked to sleep with them. The bed was very high in a dark iron frame and two long iron rods supported the light mattress full of lamb wool. She slept in the middle and put me beside her. In the afternoon they left, returning to their simple life. The departure for me was very sad and it was the first time I remember that I suffered. Every time this happened I thought, "Why can't we live all together or at least nearer to each other?" As a child you would never guess there are so many losses or separations in your life, and this may have prepared me for some of them.

Today, while writing these memories, I reflect on their lives and think how they sacrificed so much working alone on their farm and sending their own sons to live in the city to be educated, so as to have a better life.

1.4.6. June: Saint Calogero and Saint Pietro.

This month has two important native catholic feast days. Saint Calogero (Charles) is venerated by farmers for their protection and Saint Pietro (Peter) is for the protection of the fisherman. The Saccensi (the name for the Sciacca people) are very devoted to these saints' days.

The first Tuesday after Pentecost the townspeople go early in the morning to the cathedral to start the devotion called *voto* (promise)—they take off their shoes and walk bare-footed all together in a lively group, singing holy songs and reciting the rosary until they reach the church of Saint Calogero up on the mountain of the same name, about 7 kilometers away from the city. Their barefoot devotion is heart-felt as they follow the cross-bearer with bare feet praying during the entire long walk. They arrive at the church, and give thanks to the Saint for protecting their city which is subject to earthquakes.

After the ceremonies were over, people still wanted to stay together, not only in devotion but later, in fun. In the past people went on pic-nics near the church, where there is a large platform-like terrace with a small fragrant forest of pines. They celebrated with food and wine, one man played guitar, and they sang and had a good time. Once, I did the *voto* for my faith, and I found it was very touching to do.

When I think of this feast celebration, I think of my other grandpar-ents, my maternal ones. I was very young on this particular holiday. We went to their house on their own land in the mountains where they had lived all their lives together since they had started their family in this house. My grandmother, for whom I was named, was tall and skinny. She rarely talked and was very simple, quiet and neat. She cooked and cleaned and all of the other jobs were the husband's business. My *papà grande*, my grandfather, was tall and big, with a long mustache. He always had a wood pipe in his mouth, lighted or not. He smoked all day long, and when he was nervous, he smoked at night. He woke up at dawn and the tobacco odor woke up the family. I remember when he started to talk, it was usually complaining that something was wrong. He was very impulsive, and he would get up, scream, snort, and pour out his feelings. It was no use to contradict him. The family learned to ignore him and after a few minutes it was like nothing had happened. He seemed like another man. But I never saw my *nonna* (grandmother) answer him back. It was like she didn't exist there.

His nickname was *Cavaliere della Montagna* (the Mountain Cheva-lier.) They gave him that name because he talked a lot and was very friendly. When he had a glass of wine, a good time was had with every-body in the mountain where they lived, and in the city. He was modest, but he didn't care how he looked or what people thought of him.

For work and for travel to the city he had a mule. He never had a horse. He had an old female donkey, and drove the *carrozzino* (donkey cart) slowly. It was not because he could not afford it. He didn't care to take a long ride, because soon he would meet a friend and they would talk on the side of the road for half an hour, and my *mamma grande* (grandmother) would patiently wait until he would finish. My other grandparents never seemed to agree on anything. They were so different.

At the end of the month, there was another holiday, Saint Pietro. The little church dedicated to him is near the sea, at the front of the port. It was easy for the fishermen to go there to pray for their blessing. For that day, the fishermen brought the statue of Saint Peter out on a *peschereccio* (fishing boat). They would pray for a blessing og the sea, hoping to have an abundant catch that year, and all the fishermen would pray to return from the sea every night *sani e salvi* (safe and sound).

I went to see this fiesta a few times. We lived in the high side of the city, so it was not so easy for us to be there. It was not easy for my mother to take a walk so distant from our house. I went with my sister and her fiancé. We had a good time and I remember that strong fish odor near the pescherecci, walking to the navigation port.

In the afternoon after the daily rest, the young would go to see the *antenna*. This was a pole greased with soap with a flag at the end that was situated overhanging the water in the port area. A few brave boys started, trying to walk the pole to the end, but many ended up in the water. It was very difficult to do. The more fortunate and clever young men started to reach almost to the end where the grease was almost worn off. The one reaching the end and grabbing the flag was the winner and got the prize.

At night in the summer, looking up to the city from the marina, it was a spectacular sight. We admired the little old houses, with small iron balconies attached one to another. It looked like a Christmas Nativity scene. In the day, going to the marina in the full light of the afternoon, it was really a pleasure to see the arrival of the pescherecci full of fresh fish still jumping in the net, and to feel the smell of the sea water. The fish vendor was ready and filled his wood basket and started the sale yelling as loudly as possible to describe their fish as the best fresh fish—still alive. When you eat that fish you taste the marine salt and algae, a real Mediterranean taste of the Mediterranean Sea.

1.4.7. July: sun and sea.

In this hot month, there are no catholic holidays, no wonderful Sicilian traditions. The temperature is so hot that common people do not wish to celebrate. Their only wish is to go to the beach and refresh themselves in the Mediterranean water. The water is limpid, clean and the most comfortable refreshment you need in this hot month.

Sicily, situated across from Africa, is just so very hot in summer. The sun is strong, even in the early morning, and even the wind in this time is very hot. The *scirocco* (hot wind) blows hot and strong because it comes from North Africa across the water of the Mediterranean Sea. You can see the red sand that comes from the African Deserts. Thank God Sciacca has the marvelous beaches that I remember were called Stazzone, Lido, Tonnara, San Gorgio, and Capo San Marco. The water is fresh and calm. In 1950 our favorite beach was the Stazzone. We didn't have a car or bike, and in the early morning before the sunrise we had no other choice but to take a walk to the nearest beach to us, the Stazzone.

I remember the walk went like this. After a few tortuous little steep streets, finally we see the beach, and we start to unbutton our clothes to be ready to get into that clean water. The sand is fine and very pleasant to take a nap on after our swim, or to take a walk, after liberating our feet from our uncomfortable shoes. We understand the pleasure of walking barefoot of the fishermen, first because he loved the feel of the sand, second because it was easier, and then maybe sometimes for relief from new shoes!

Across from the sea there are a few little old houses which the fishermen used for their work many years ago, fixing the nets, or for storage. Now some fortunate people own them and use them for summer vacations. Some people rent them for a couple of summer months. Today, little by little, they are opening a few restaurants near the beach, with coffee shops and some amusements for children, and now it has become a very busy place.

I think the majority of the people prefer the beach in the heat of the summer, but a few people prefer the mountains. My mother was one of them. She preferred to stay seated under a tree (especially the *Carruba* or Carob) with its large, round branches, and stay cool. She crocheted, read a book, or better yet, took a nap in the fresh mountain wind.

1.4.8. August: *Ferragosto.*

This is the really hot month of the year. The city is full of tourists. The emigrants return to see their families and friends, and to pass a nice and carefree vacation. The city starts to prepare for the holiday of the *Madonna del Soccorso*. The vendors start to prepare their own wagons to show their merchandise, yelling to advertise their best quality and good prices.

The *Madonna del Soccorso* is the city patron. The statue is of heavy Carrara marble, representing Maria with Jesus in her arms, and a bat (ready to defend the city). For three days, August 13th, 14th, and 15th, it is like a city in heaven. On the morning of the 15th, the people start to celebrate the *Santa Messa* (Saint's Mass). At 1:00 there is the festive dinner. The men always went to see the horse races (*corsa dei cavalli*). My father loved this race, and we went a few times. They are just for fun, not for money, and the winning horse and rider get a prize.

At night, the *Madonna* statue is transported by barefoot fishermen, and pushed by two long poles and mounted on a platform. A group of fishermen pull the heavy statue, and she is transported through all the city streets this way. The first stop is always to bless the sea and then the city streets. Every few blocks they stop and everyone shouts, *"Viva Maria!"* In the meantime, they try to relax under the heavy load. The municipal band plays the appropriate Catholic songs. Some people recite the rosary or sing the *Ave Maria*. At the end, all the people are tired and hot, and they search for a place to sit in an outside coffee shop, to get refreshed with a cool lemon *granita* (lemon ice, see recipe section 3.3.13), or bitter and sweet tasting fruit *gelato* (ice cream) made of many fruits or other ingredients.

The teenagers walked up and down in the piazza, and they used to eat the *calia e simenza* (sunflower and watermelon seeds and roasted beans) from a brown paper cone. For a few coins you could be chewing all night. We listened to the band playing operatic arias. At 12:00 midnight we would start to hear the first noise from the fireworks exploding in the air. It was always special at the end when it was the noisiest! This is the expected sign for people that the religious party is over.

So we finally returned home, walking because we did not own a car. On the way, we saw the watermelon vendor wagon standing in the side of the street waiting for customers. With a small amount of money, you could taste a lot of pieces of melons. After finding the right taste for you, you would buy the melon and bring it home to eat. We would sit on the balcony and continue to eat the melon, and gossip about the things we saw that day.

(I remember that years ago when a boyfriend did not want to wait until the wedding day to make love, the insulted girl would answer, "Do you think I am like a piece of melon? If you like the taste you must buy it!" Back then, virginity was really the first thing the bride would bring to the husband. She deserved to wear that white dress and veil. It was a symbol of virginity!).

We slept a few hours, and at sunrise we were ready again for the *scampagnata* (picnic). The next day, we would go to the farm to take it easy, tired from the fiesta.

1.4.9. September: the grape harvest.

Vinu di Sciacca, nettari prelibatu tu sulu po' aggiustari, stu munnu scunc-intratu ("The wine of Sciacca, like sweet nectar, that can only can set the disorganized world right.") Indeed, these are the words of the famous poet Vincenzo Licata. With just a few glasses of wine, and just for a few moments, it makes one think that the world is perfect, and makes one feel so knowledgeable.

Wine for the Sicilian is the right drink to celebrate any happy event. With a toast, a Sicilian will raise his glass and express his feelings, with a word from the heart, he will exclaim *salute!* (To your health).

In vino veritas, (in wine, truth!) like when A. Manzoni wrote in his book, <u>The Promised Spouse,</u> that the young groom, Renzo, told the truth, hurting the bride's family's reputation. He asked to be excused for this hurt, saying that it was not he who talked, but the wine that talked for him!

I remember the harvest of the first grapes as the first real memory I have of my father. The vineyard was truly his paradise! The first week of September the farmers always started to check the grapes to see if they were ripening. He tells if they are ripe when they start to develop a distinct musty odor. Soon the time is right for the harvest, and in the early morning, with knife and basket, it starts.

My father would go out with his large straw hat covering his head from the sun, still very hot in September. With his basket and knife ready for his happy adventure, he is helped by my grandfather, my uncle and a few young strong friends. The grapes seem like they are hiding under the large leaves. Everyone begins to cut the ripe bunches and fill the baskets. The girls are ready to help to bring the baskets home, emptying them into a large vat, and in the meantime, they are singing happy country songs and teasing each other, for they do not fear the fierce sun and the hard work.

Soon the vat was full, and two big young men wearing large heavy shoes with soles full of round nails got inside of the big vat. They jumped like they were dancing, and crushed the grapes, like it was a joke. The air was perfumed with the sweet aroma of the grapes. Everybody participated in that happy, extraordinary event. Even the numerous wasps wanted to participate, trying to give a nasty sting to the participants (I know!). This was the start of the traditional grape harvest which has been mostly mechanized today.

After that first crush, the pressing job was passed to the animals using a large stone pushed by a mule with side blinders so he would not get dizzy. The work continued until as much as possible was squeezed. The juice went to one vat and the pulp was separated into another, each with further uses.

Working all day, my father finally started to put the juice into the barrels, which had been carefully prepared beforehand. I remember seeing my father the week before preparing the old wood barrel treating them with a sulfuric bath **and** putting a candle inside the empty barrel so that the light shining from the hole could be seen, inside the empty barrel (this was good for drying).

"PINCH" OF SICILY

A COLLECTION OF MEMORIES
AND TRADITIONAL RECIPES

By
Maria Sciortino

I watched him perform it right. I didn't understand what he was doing or why, but I was sure that in a few months it would become a delicious outstanding wine. Our wine was rosé. The quality grapes from our vineyard were almost all The *Nzolia* and *Catarrattu* (Inzolia and Catarratto) varieties. It is very good for a rosé wine. The *Zibibbo* (sweet white grape) we used to eat with bread, our summer lunch.

After so much ritual and care, finally on November 11th, Saint Martin's Day came. "*A San Martino, ogni mosto diventa vino*" (At Saint Martin's Day, all grape juice becomes wine.") Now we were ready for opening the barrel for the first time. A rubber pipe sucks from the hole until the wine comes into the mouth, and then the pipe is put in the bottle to fill it, ready to taste. The good new wine was our "*bonjule novu*". My father would proudly relish the new wine, really full of life and happiness. That was one of the best days of the year. Raise the glass with me: *salute* to my father!

1.4.10. October: clouds

We look at the sky, and the clouds promise to bring a welcome rain, to refresh the humid, hot summer air. In fact, in Sicily in the summer it almost never rains. The soil is arid, and almost radiates dust. The grasses are yellow and brown, thorny and woody. The only way to purify the soul from this is a fire in the dried brush, but today it is very dangerous to do that, so everyone prepares for a good rain, to start to clean and make ready new soil. Finally the dark clouds come and they bring the welcome rain. The water touches the dried soil, and produces a red tinted dust. The farm people happily look outside, ready the next day to start to plow in the early morning, or hoe by hand, or use a plow pulled by a mule. They will make better, large furrows, and make the soil ready for new seeding. When I was young, Sicilian agriculture was based on the *frumento* (wheat). This was the most important harvest.

The *mulini* (mills) ground the flour making it ready for delicious fresh breads and pastas.

My mother was an expert make *macarruna* (pastas) by hand. At every family occasion she was ready to do it, and we never appreciated all of the good things she did all of the time. But we all ate willingly.

Today I know it is too late to say thank you to her. Only after I became a parent did I start to understand what my parents did for me! And they dif it quietly, with so much love. Unfortunately, life is like a fast run that pushes us so fast to the finish line, not giving us the time to look back, reflect, and to see if we skipped some piece of the road that was important, but we didn't see it, or value it.

When we finally look back, it is too late to understand what we may have lost, and like a string of rich pearls, we try to retrieve and conserve it like a precious family treasure for our children and grandchildren.

1.4.11. November: sorrow and joy.

The first day of the month is All Saints Day. It is everybody's *onomastico* (name day). All the people exchange with each other their best wishes. The second day is for the deceased, *I morti* (the dead). Everyone goes to church for the Mass offered in memory of their own dear deceased. We take walks to the cemetery to bring flowers and candles to the graves and tombs. Some are buried in the ground, covered with a marble headstone inscribed with their names, and some are encased in the various cemetery chapels.

My grandfather always pondered the afterlife, wondering about so many things. While he still worked he started to prepare for the eternal life house. He bought some land in the cemetery, big enough to construct a chapel. Every time he found a good stone he would put it aside. After he accumulated many stones he rented a truck and sent them to the cemetery to use in the construction. After a few years, he started to build the chapel large enough for eight people. Today they rest in peace, my grandparents in the center, the two sons on the sides and the daughters-in-law near their husbands. Because he was a strong and hard-working man, I think he made it possible for the family to stay together for eternity.

For the day of the deceased, the people stayed in the cemetery all day honoring their loved ones memories and looking at their pictures. In Sicily it is really touching to see the pictures of loved ones on each of the tombs. A lot of the time, the photos were taken before they were elderly, so they look young and healthy. That day is for dedicating and remembering the dead who have left us.

But in the night…the sorrowful day becomes a joyful event for the children.

Yes, indeed! That is a really special night for the young. For us, November 2nd is like Christmas night. That night, the *morti* (deceased person) become our Santa Claus bringing presents: toys, clothes, sweets and many other things. If we have been good all year the *morti* bring us presents, but if we have been bad he tickles our feet. I tried to remember: what did I do, good or bad? I was terrified all night. I tried to keep my feet tight inside the sheets. Thankfully, they never tickled me. Finally the next morning came, and under the bed or in the corner I would find a basket full of *frutti Matturana* (marzipan, see recipe section 3.3.18). It is sugar and almond paste in the shape of fruits, so naturally they are a culinary work of art. In the middle of the basket would be a sugar dolly for the girls and a sugar horse for the boys. But we can't eat any yet…oh no! First, we must put it on display to show off what we received to friends and relatives. But we manage to nibble a few pieces from the back to eat when no one sees us, until the statue does not stand up anymore. Only then are we allowed to eat it, when it was dried and stale

One year I received a real play doll. I named her Rita. I played with her, but I was afraid to look into her eyes because they moved around. For a few years, it was the same toy, but one year, before the *morti*, my doll disappeared. Then that morning I received Rita in a different outfit and hat my sister had sewn. I was so happy to see her again and happy to receive anything, no matter what it was.

As far as toys, I remember I never had a bicycle and never learned to ride one. My brothers had one for the both of them, the only one they ever had. My young brother sometimes would give me a ride. He would pedal and I would sit on the front handle bars…I felt so lucky.

One year was so special. This was when I knew who really brought the toys (but I made believe I didn't!). I received a little dining room set, so pretty with drawers that really opened glasses, dishes and cups, and a table and chairs. This was the most beautiful present for me. I treated it so gently. I took care and enjoyed playing with it for many years.

Since that time, dishes, glasses and cups became my favorite pieces of home furnishings. For me, the dining room is the most cozy, lovely and enjoyable corner of my home.

1.4.12. December: *Natale* (Christmas)

This is the most beautiful holiday of the year. But the temperature is frigidly cold. The snows already cover the mountains. Some athletic people who live in the city travel to the distant, steep White Mountains. Mount Etna is ready to visit and have fun skiing, for that feeling of freedom on the snow in that white paradise. In my family we didn't play sports. For the girls there was nothing! It was not permitted for the girls because our place was to stay home to sew or study, and practice being a lady! The only sport my younger brother played was the game of soccer, popular all over Italy.

The Catholic holidays started on December 8th with the *Immacolata Concezione* (Immaculate Conception Day). It was celebrated in the church with a solemn procession. December 13, Santa Lucia, was the Catholic religion and more traditional family event. The night before, the Sicilian ladies start to put the grain and the seeds in to soak and be ready to cook the next day. The *cuccìa* (soup of grain, like cuscus), was served with a sweet syrup of *vino cotto* (cooked wine). An old Sicilian legend says that the people, in devotion to St. Lucia (patroness of the eyes) on this day should prefer to eat the cuccìa all day, and not any bread.

On December 16th, the Christmas *novena* starts—the church prepares for the birth of the Baby Jesus with prayers and nativity songs like "*Tu scendi dalle stele*" (You come from the stars) for nine days—in anticipation of the Nativity.

My family would start to prepare the Christmas cookies. For a couple of days our house was a mess from flour, sugar, *marmellata di fichi* (fig marmalade, prepared the summer before), and ready to make the *cucciddrati* (Sicilian fig cookies with a sugar cookie dough). The work was hard because it required a lot of attention and practice to be able to execute the tiny designs in the dough. My mother started the wood oven, and my sister gave the cookies the finishing touch, and in a short time this cookie was ready to be eaten on the special day.

December 24th in the afternoon, all the fish stores were empty. All the fish available was in the family kitchens ready to be cooked. Every family had different ways to cook, or celebrate the day.

In our family the first tradition was to cook *baccalà a la ghiotta* (salt-cured cod, see recipes section). It was soaked, and the water changed every day. After a week, finally the fish smelled good, and was ready to be cooked. My mother, the model wife, all afternoon tried to prepare my father's favorite meals. Another fish that never missed on our table was the *insalata di polpo* (octopus salad, see recipe section). Everything that night is based on fish, because the Christmas vigil is a time to abstain from meat.

On December 25, the bell start to ring early, announcing "JESUS IS BORN—come to church to adore Him". We got ready, dressed in heavy wool coats (despite a warmer day, to be stylish) and went to church where we greeted our friends and wished them Merry Christmas. We returned home, where the table was festively set, and the succulent food was waiting for us. *Buon Natale a tutti* (Merry Christmas to all).

1.5. DISCUSSIONS IN SICILY

Our use of argument, our heated discussions, can be compared to music. Sometimes it is symphonic, sometimes like *opera*, and sometimes dramatic. Every town, even those a few kilometers away, has different customs and different ways of doing things, and a dialect with different words. In Sicily there exists an absolute *campanilismo* ("one's own hometown is best" kind of boasting). Perhaps because people do not have much to do or think about, they dedicate themselves to defending their particular culture. It all begins with a discussion with someone who comes from another town, perhaps only a ten minute automobile trip away.

"My town is the biggest and most modern in Sicily. It has the biggest and most extraordinary thing in the whole world—none can say it is its equal."

One continues the discussion full of nothing (and lies) until one is tired. The outcome is the "white flag". It is not easy but if you give up, you'll win. If you don't—it will continue until tomorrow, sipping on coffee and calling on friends to continue the discussion.

Perhaps the above is exaggerated, but it is so in Sicily where the talks of *campanilismo* revolve about soccer and politics. When the discussion begins, everyone is an expert. Everyone is better informed and no one is ever wrong!!! Sicilians speak in three ways—with the Heart—with their Hands—and with the Tongue. When we are sentimental we know how to talk with the Heart. If we are angry, the Hands speak more that the mouth. If there is a discussion that is less important, then we use the Tongue—just to talk.

1.6. MUSIC AND OPERA

I don't think there is anyone in the world who does not love music—young old and even babies. Each has his own rhythm in his heart. There is no need for special words or sophisticated instruments. Each sound or melody touches the heart.

Italians are all heart, food and music.

I remember my father (before television), seated on the lounge chair on the balcony, listening to the radio—we had a GM radio victrola. He enjoyed listening to the _Stornellate_ by Onofrio e Caterina, an Italian-American couple that sang songs and told jokes. Many years later, when I was walking along 16th Avenue and 75th Street in Brooklyn, NY, my aunt pointed out their beautiful house. I remembered how my father enjoyed listening to them.

I began listening to opera while seated on the balcony of our house. Each evening, an old gentleman, with the title _Cavaliere_ (honored gentleman), who lived across from us, would sit on his balcony listening to opera until very late. Even if I was already in bed, I would listen to those sweet melodies. At that time I did not know what I was listening to, but already knew that I liked it. When I heard Madam Butterfly or La Boheme, I would dream with my eyes wide open.

I began to recognize the names of the operas, the tenors and sopranos—Renata Tebaldi, Franco Corelli and Maria Meneghini Callas—"The Divine". At the time, she was overweight and had started to diet. There were always bitter rivalries. The newspapers always reported gossip about these stars—but no one could deny their excellence—their golden voices.

Even Sicily would boast of having a Great Maestro. Our Vincenzo Bellini—with the famous opera Norma. He was immortalized in Catania with a part bearing his name. Italy has had great conductors and great tenors—from the great Caruso to Luciano Pavarotti. I enjoy listening to _Elisir d'amore_ and Turandot. When Pavarotti sings _Vincerà_, his magical voice is enhanced by the acoustics of the Metropolitan. It touches me profoundly—as it does the entire audience.

Music like love, speaks a universal language.

1.7. FASHION

One of the prime human necessities has always been to dress oneself to cover and protect the body. But as history has recorded, from the beginning of time and especially in the 20th century, more became expected. Everyone wanted something unique and individualistic. In the past, each social class dressed in a specific way. Everyone copied others to appear equal or more elegant than the other—even to extreme and strange styles.

I began to understand and follow styles in 1951 by looking at fashion magazines. I remember one designer, Shubert, who was a short man full of courage. Another designer I knew was the stylist Pucci.

The first fashion show I knew of was with the most elegant client of Dior, the richly decorated Marchese of Florence. This first fashion show was organized in his own home with the label "Made in Italy". Then he continued each year at the Pitti Palace. One could admire the new styles shown beautifully by wonderful models.

With television, we admired the styles of actresses and singers, and we all copied them—especially the singer Mina. I would copy her clothes, hair styles and accessories. Most of the girls wore the same styles. It was the era of the "tailored look"—gloves, hats, purses and spiked heels—a regular cut showing a protruding bust line and narrow waist—like Sophia Loren or Gina Lollobrigida—with their curly hair—the style was called *tira baci*.

Today, Italy is full of stylists of the highest order—really make "Made in Italy" is about a fashion paradise. With sophisticated models, an expert artisan professional—such as my husband—who works with his hands, patience and courage, takes a single piece of material and turns it into a piece of art.

Today's styles are so different. So many of the styles favor *nudismo*. Young models are encouraged to be thinner and more muscular. Hopefully designers like Giorgio Armani will bring back those beautiful models, when a woman can return to her mysterious look and be really impeccably beautiful.

1.8. SORROW

For me, sorrow is the death of my father, the man I loved so much, with whom I was so similar in character. It is also the loss of my husband's parents. The tragic loss of my younger sister and brother-in-law, a couple who left behind their children. I remember when my grandparents died and the loss of a good family friend. It is knowing there are hungry people in the world. And most of all, sorrow is to me the tears of your family and knowing you cannot dry those tears.

My greatest sorrow was the loss of my dear mother. I was so sorry for my father. The death of my mother was so profound because she died in my arms. I can admit now that I remained traumatized for a long time after that. I would ask myself, how could it be that the person who gave me life, that protected me like a shield all my life has now left me? When the terrible day of her passing came, she took a piece of me with her. I never had expected that her absence would leave such a hole in my heart. It was a few months before my sixtieth birthday, but I still felt young. The passing of my mother felt more of a life change than when I went through menopause.

The day my mother was gone I felt as if all my years had caught up to me in one day. I was no longer the daughter, but now I became the mother and grandmother. I no longer had someone to go and visit for help, now I became the shield for the family. It was a big commitment. One consolation was that she said before she died how blessed she felt that God allowed her to die with her children near. Today she rests in peace near her beloved, my father, proud that she was a good wife, and more, a sweet Mother.

1.9. DEPARTURE

There was a song I heard a long time ago which had the words: *partire che tristezza, lasciare che dolore* (depart with sadness, leave with pain).

From the time I heard that song sung, it made me so sad to think what leaving could be. I wanted to stay with my family and friends all the time. I never dreamed about *partire* (leaving).

My first experience with "leaving" began with my grandparents—everytime they left to go to their home on the farm only a short distance away—and knowing that I would not see them for a week made me think—why do they have to live so far away. Why can't we live near each other so we can see each other and be together all the time?

Our town was small; all we had was an elementary and high school, not a college. My brother was the first to go to college. But he had to leave our small town and go to Palermo where he would live while going to college. For him it was a beautiful experience—being by himself to live in the city, study, go out with his friends and have his own freedom. For our family it was very sad—he was the first to leave the family. I remember my mother preparing his clothes and food—almost like he was going to another world. For me it was scary—would I see him again? When? The first time he left it was devastating for me. After a few weeks he came home. Almost everytime he came home, he would bring me a book and I it made me so happy. Each time he went away I would be sad, but would be happy when he came back—and bring me another book.

A few years later, my father started going to Palermo with my brother to work and stay there for a week at a time. The night before he would leave, he would prepare a suitcase and my heart would begin to palpitate because I did not want him to go. I never said anything, not even to my sister—but in my own silence I would always ask why. One time my father took me with him to Palermo. I was so excited. We left at 6 o'clock in the morning and took the bus. At that time they had not yet constructed the *autostrada* (super highway). We traveled through many small towns, along many dusty roads, around a lot of curves and mountains. The bus smoked and had a strong odor from the smelly gas. But for me it was an extraordinary experience. I would think wistfully about my mother and my sister at home, but the curiosity to see a new city made me strong.

Finally after 6 hours of traveling, we arrived at the station near Via Maqueda. When we left the bus I remember I was so excited. I was attracted to all of the window displays, the colored signs on the store fronts, and the neon lights. There was a tram (electric bus) with their electric lines that seemed to be suspended from the sky. After my father finished his business he took me to a department store. In the store, for the first time, I saw an escalator—what an invention—moving stairs. For a few seconds, I was afraid to put my foot on the step. But then we were on the second floor. I never saw a store with a second floor—in our little town all the stores were on one level—with simple displays. In Palermo there were beautiful displays in two department stores, called Standa and Upim. How wonderful they were!

My father bought me a handbag. It was my most favorite accessory. I had already felt that I had seen the world. It would have been even more beautiful if my mother and sister had been there with me.

My father went back and forth from our town to Palermo for several years. And still every time he left I felt sad. I never dreamed that one day I would leave my family and my homeland to experience what *partenza* (parting) really means, alone with my husband, leaving everything behind. But I did it.

Forty years have passed and thank God, I have good health and a good life with my husband, sons and their families. I missed my family so much, especially on the holidays or some other events that I would have loved to share with them. Now I have grandchildren and I feel that I never want to leave them. But reluctantly when the weather turns cold in New York, my husband and I go to Florida where it is warm. Some say that I am lucky—but I think it is my destiny to leave.

I have never had complete happiness—I realize that I always have to pay the price of it and have to sacrifice something else, in order to have a good thing.

1.10. HAPPINESS.

Happiness is:

Having a good life companion, on whom you can lean on in traumatic moments.

Having good children, feeling proud to bring them into life.

Hearing your children calling you *mamma*.

Seeing your children have their own children.

Becoming a grandmother.

Being healthy and peaceful.

Giving a hand to someone who has fallen.

Loving all people like yourself.

Participating in keeping peace in your family and in the world.

Seeing all people have their own ray of sunshine.

Having freedom and respect for one another.

Living a long and healthy life to enjoy future family generations.

1.11. THE TROUSSEAU.

Having a daughter in Sicily was a happy event for the mother. She would have a girl all her life near her for everything the family needed. The daughter is there ready to help the mother. For the father, it is a happy event when she is born, but when she gets older, he must begin to prepare "*la dota*" (the dowry). The mother starts to crochet lace tablecloths and napkins and kitchen cloths, making sure that everything is coordinated. She begins to prepare her trousseau. The family (depending on their wealth) begins to decide how many sets of linen, underwear, blankets, jewelry etc. They get busy buying, embroidering and showing off the large trousseau that the girl will have for a wedding present. Soon the engagement is announced, and all the family and friends already know what the fiancé would have from the father. If the family is *benestanti*—rich—she would have a house for a gift and a good amount of money. If the family was middle class, the father would promise an abundant clothing set (trousseau) and a list of what he would pay for the wedding.

It is easier for the girl to marry young, because when the girl gets older (in her 20's) the girl would be known as a *zitella* or spinster. So the family starts to show off or tell everybody what the girl will bring to a future husband.

At the engagement the couple exchange rings—the family gets together for a big dinner and all is in perfect harmony. Every *passeggiata* (walk) by the couple is accompanied by all of the family-the many chaperones make it look like a procession. The family must watch the girl to make sure that they do not kiss or "something else" could happen. Then really she could never marry.

Soon the time of the wedding arrives. A few weeks before the family starts to prepare the invitations. Some people deserve a special invitation, and so they take the invitation by hand to be sure that they are received. They prepare the *dota* to show all the family and friends and all those that are curious. They put the *biancheria* (clothing) all over the rooms. The invited people bring presents of their own taste (at that time no registry existed) or they bring money. All the presents are displayed on the table with the people's names—even all the money (lire). Everybody looks, especially the boy's family—at the magnificent or miserable trousseau that the girl has.

What now you ask? And what does the man bring? If the father has property, the father gives them a piece of land, or a job so the family is reassured of good work so that he can support his wife like a "signora" so that she can stay home like a lady.

The family reminds the friends and family that they have invited to make sure to be there at the wedding. Sometimes the invited say they are not sure they can come, and then they start the game for they want to be "begged" to come. But sometimes the pre-wedding happiness becomes litigation between the girl and the boy's family. They start to fight over missed money or expected gifts—what the father promised at the time of the engagement. To marry his daughter he promises much—but when the time comes, sometimes he cannot afford it and there is trouble. The fathers argue and the boy and girl want to break off the engagement (or they make believe they want to). The girl cries, the girl's mother talks to the boy's mother and they talk to their husbands. Even some well respected people talk to the girl's father and persuade him to calm down—give some more and guarantee the wedding will happen. Because if the wedding does not happen, it would be very hard for the girl to find another boy to marry her. The father calms down, signs some more notes and they try their best to celebrate the wedding. This is, of course, a tale of the past.

The father brings the daughter to the altar and the mother cries to see her own baby already married. In the reception hall, all the guests applaud the first dance—the best man makes the toast and all cheer. And all those who were not so sure they could come are the first in line with their children and grandchildren and neighbors. The bride and groom are happy and pass out the confetti, and the waiters run back and forth distributing cookies, ice cream cups and the glass of *rosolio,* a homemade cordial—and everyone drinks from the same glass. Each person drinks, puts back the glass on the tray and the waiter refills it and the next person drinks from it—no one was concerned about germs then.

The family is happy to see the newlyweds kiss and go on their honeymoon and they wonder if she will have a girl or a boy. The bride is sure it will be a girl and the groom stubbornly insists that it will be a boy.

1.12. THE BABY'S NAME.

Soon they know that the girl has pregnant since the first month of marriage. Now what will the name of the first baby be? If it is a boy, it is the paternal father's name, if it is a girl it is the paternal mother's name. The *erede* (the first boy's name) is very important, since he will carry on the family name. Sometimes the family continues to name other children after the aunts and uncles living or deceased—but that was not as important. This is much discussed and they are obligated for the first child, otherwise the baby for life will have angry grandparents—with the baby not at fault—and will have to suffer the consequences.

I heard a story a few years ago—An Italian industrialist's son married an Israeli girl. Soon they found out that she would have a baby and everyone was happy. The Italian father-in-law was happy but worried that the daughter-in-law might have different traditions with naming the baby. He called the his son's wife aside and said to her "Listen to me well—you have two choices: your son can be a rich Giuseppe or a poor David. It is your choice. There is no middle ground." At the christening the grandfather was very happy to have a grandson named Giuseppe, and quickly set up a bank account to accumulate money for the grandson for college.

Today, thinking about that it seems so strange to reason and talk like that. Every tradition has a sort dictatorial aspect but really calls for respecting old ideas. Certainly everybody would love to have his own name continued but the more important thing is that the baby is in good health. We should be happy for the beautiful name they have and proud to see them continuing to enlarge and enrich the family.

1.13. MEALS AND FRIENDS.

My husband and I have many friends in common. Some are very special—we get together to talk about our own joy and problems and share our free time just to joke and share our own ideas. Everyone expresses his own opinion and says what they think while trying to not hurt anybody. We are all nearly the same age. We don't feel like we are aged and we don't like to hear about it. We think aging just doesn't fit us! We all try to feel, or better to look, young and full of life, especially the women, who try to look better all the time in all ways. As our friend Angelo says, "One woman's hair could support the Verrazzano Narrows Bridge!"

Even the men play their own part but in a different, more quiet and controlled way. They approach everything with their own persistence. It's beautiful to talk with a friend, and to understand each other. Friendship makes life richer and is something indispensable. It is beautiful to think that after family you still have somebody to count on.

Sciacca has a special affection for having *schiticchiu* (outdoor meals with friends). People frequently take their daily walks through the piazza (*lu chianu*), up and down and down and up, sometimes for hours and hours, especially on the cold winter nights when they need to do something different and are tired of being inside. So soon they see a friend, invite him to call other friends, and each puts in a little money and they buy a few pounds of fish or sausage. Another friend might come with abundant olive oil. Some of the women would start to boil the pasta, some would prepare accompanying condiments. One of the most preferred is Pasta al Pesto (see recipe section) with olive oil, garlic, and basil, ground in a mortar with a pestle to become a most tasty *pasta con salsa* you would want to eat.

Between every dish, people make a toast (*brindisi*) and drink a glass with their close friends, and one by one everyone takes turn toasting each other and then it becomes a loud party. Today everybody, men and women, can participate, but in olden times, just the men could participate, because sometimes they would get drunk and start talking loud and dirty in front of the women. So the men would prefer going off by themselves and doing whatever they wanted while their wives would be waiting at home. (This was justified by saying that the husband works so he has the right to go off with other men) The husband would come home later in the night, singing and drunk, and so many times a battle would start in the family. Today there if there is a party, all the family goes together to have a good time, to spend the evening with a friend, and finish it with a coffee and a small pastry prepared by some expert cook or with Sicilian *cannoli* to conclude the magnificent *serata*, or evening out.

1.14. MY PARENTS.

My mother has two sisters and one young brother. From an early age, because she was the older daughter, she stayed home and helped her mother with domestic housework. She did go to school until the third grade but she couldn't even go every day. Because she was a girl, she was supposed to stay home and take care of the family, and clean and cook. Back then they thought that education for girls wasn't really important because one day she would marry and the husband would take care of everything. But my mother loved to go to school and she loved the young modern teacher and talking to her and she loved to look at the modern clothes she wore. She also loved hear and see things she had never known before. For my mother it was like she was discovering a new world around her.

However, this beautiful time ended in a few years. She continued to learn when her sister did her homework for she tried to copy her. Her sister went to school for only a few more years more than she did.

From the time that she was very young, her father tried to find a good man for her to marry. Once she married, the father would have no more worries. Then the husband would take care of her. She would be a married woman and she would be settled. This traditional view about love was that if they were not in love before the marriage, it would come later, with time!

Before she was even fourteen years old, a friend introduced his son to her father. The fathers talked, and in a few years, when they grew up a little more, they planned to be engaged. But the boy didn't do well, so the engagement was called off (Thank God because my mother was not happy, as he wasn't her choice!). Soon the parents started to look for somebody else.

From a *comare* (godmother) they met another boy who was recommended and he came from a good family. They were at the same level in property and class. And as soon as my mother was sixteen years old, after the discussion about the *dota* (dowry-property and wedding gifts from the bride's family), she was promised to be engaged to this twenty year-old man. And luckily, as soon as my mother saw him, she fell in love. She knew nothing about him, and had not ever seen him before, and yet she was happy (thank God).

Once a week the fiancé would go visit the girl's family, to shake hands and to give her a smile (she was almost afraid just to do that). From the first moment the fiancé came into the house, he would talk to the prospective father-in-law, and gave a smile once in a while to the girl who was seated near her mother (properly far from him) and she was always happy to see him.

My father's family was very rigid and composed. He has a brother that is much younger. My father's father worked on the farm, but he preferred for his children to have an education. My father attended and finished the elementary school class and after he was an adult he completed the night school class, the so called *avviamento professionale*. He could read and write very well and he loved mathematics. He became a *sensale* (food salesman). He was always elegant and perfect, and he would speak a little and then continue to respond with a half smile. He had his mother's charisma; he was older and friendly. But because of his very strict and rigorous father, he learned to be strong and very deep and he was really a serious man from the time that he was young.

After a short engagement they got married . My mother was seventeen and my father twenty-one. They lived together with my father's parents. The young bride was happy, for she lived in their home like she was another daughter, and the mother-in-law loved her. Little by little, after so much obedience and love for her husband, she realized that she was really the wife, and a mother. They lived together for ten years until his brother married and they left the rooms for the new couple. Older now, she had her own home and life became a little better still, but always she under her husband's control-her husband was the family captain. She never really became the lady of the house: she obeyed all her life and happily approved everything the husband decided.

They had four children two boys, two girls, and I am the youngest. I never heard my parents talk about anything important in front of us. Even when they discussed something with relatives they sent us to play in another room, and we just had to spy through the cracks!

Those were what I call the "Accepting Years." Children had to accept everything the parents said with no objection!

Sometimes we felt angry with them, but we realized that we had to obey, and we are trained to do it. Young parents had to look like strong teachers in front of their children, even though they are soft people. The parents had one important rule. My grandfather used to say, "Only kiss and hug the children when they are asleep. Do not demonstrate a lot of love. It was necessary not to spoil them, so that they will learn well." With my sister and brothers, my parents were very tough and much more rigorous. I was born later, in a more modern time, and with me it was easier to have a discussion. I tried to get closer to them, to talk to them about some matters, and we were able to talk more confidently together, but just a little, and not like I really wanted.

My older brother was very restless and intelligent, and in everything he wanted to understand more and more. I was interested in everything he said, in all his modern ideas for his discoveries interested me very much. I tried to imitate him. My younger brother was different, so happy and playful, so tall and skinny, a blonde with blue eyes, elegant, with a style that was much admired. My sister was so good and serious. The relationship with her was as if she were my younger mother. I talk to her of all my problems and she taught me sewing and embroidery, and how to act like a lady. I hid the first cosmetics I ever used from her. I tried to mirror everything she did, but I had to wait until I was a teenager to use makeup, wear nylon panty hose, or high heel shoes (although I already had a boy who liked me, I felt ashamed that I still looked like a little girl). My sister stayed engaged for ten years. Her fiancé Paolo was the older son of a large family. He got work, helped the family, and waited a few years for the marriage of his older sister.

In the meantime my father was not in good shape financially. In fact his business status changed when his mill with the old machinery that ground the grain for the farmers had to close. In those days the whole wheat, which we did not recognize was the best part, went to one side to be sold cheap, and it was used to feed chickens. The white flour was all starch, and was sold to make bread at home.

For a long time the mill had done very well, but when the technology changed, new electrically advanced mills came and produced much finer, extra white flour. New machines made *pasta* also, and no one had to make it by hand any longer. So the old small businesses were closed.

For a few years he tried to find a job, but he wasn't so young anymore. He tried to start another business for a few years with my younger brother. Like most people in Sicily who had problems like this, he began to think about emigrating.

In the fifties, my sister was engaged and the couple never went out alone. Some family member, or sometimes all of the family, would follow them. I was her only sister (my mother never went out to have a good time) and so I was often the person in charge of watching them. In Sicily the person in charge was called "the person who keeps the candle." Years ago when they didn't have electricity, one person in the family would make sure that they keep the light on to make sure nothing happened. I was instructed by my mother that they should not even have one kiss. Well, I was alert to watch for this, yet sometimes I saw them hug or kiss. I was embarrassed, so I made believe that I wasn't looking at that particular moment. Finally they happily married.

I was engaged a few years later, but still I couldn't take a walk with my fiancé alone, as I was watched by my mother or a friend. I was engaged for a couple of years, and thanks to going to America, we didn't have to wait as long as she did.

All of my siblings and I, while we were single, were united and close. But when we married, just my sister remained in the city, and the three of us went to live in other places, and I went the most distant of all, to another country.

Thanks to letters, phone calls, and annual visits, we tried to keep in touch. I talk so much about all my family…and…I…who do I resemble?

My husband observed that I am nothing like my mother. My mother agreed with my father in everything. She always just said, "Defend your man, right or wrong." I think differently; I am more open, and more liberal. My mother supported everything my father said or did. Not me, for me right is right and wrong is wrong, no matter who you are. I think I inherited my father's charisma, I came from that part of the family breaddough. I was born and grew up by the Mediterranean too. Since I was very young, I learned to cover my feelings, my weaknesses, and to appear cool and strong. But sometimes I didn't follow that example!

I grew up, emigrated, matured in a different time and culture, and little by little I learned to be myself…I learned to express the love, the affection, and the weaknesses in me. When I became a mother I really knew about wanting to hug and kiss my sons! I liked what I read in Jimmy Durante's memoir, which said: "Even the boys need caressing, they need to see the parents' love." He never saw that, because he had cold parents. He also said, "Even men can cry." That was prohibited in his own time. With time even my father changed a little. In his old age he was so sweet with his grandchildren…but he never spoiled them. Because of the example of many generations before, it was not so easy to change this part of his lifestyle.

This change was the best…now we can hug and kiss frequently. This was the best thing to happen to our family. Now I hope to live longer to give my children and grandchildren all the hugs and kisses that many old great-great grandmothers for generations before wanted to give to us.

I hope to see my grandchildren grow up and see my face full of wrinkles because of the many laughs that I hope we will have together.

1.15. MY TEACHERS.

I have always had the utmost respect for teachers. I loved to have a teacher near me to talk with, ask questions and receive the right answer.

My first teacher was my brother, who gave me my first book "Your Friend Jesus". It was a small Bible that taught me to read and to love. I still have that little precious book.

When I attended elementary school, I had the same teacher for five years. The teacher was an older woman, who was very religious, very strict and completely dedicated to the education of the children she taught. With patience and love, through her first lessons, she taught me the fundamentals of life.

For me she was like a second mother. She was the person that I was supposed to listen to, after my parents. The students, all girls, loved and respected her, firstly because she was absolutely perfect and secondly because school was our second home, where we would live and learn and also learn to be obedient. There were some days when we would not be so happy being at school. But we could not go home and expect support from our parents because the answer from our parents would be "the teacher is your educator and she has the right to be strict. We learned to be quiet and to listen to her. So even if there were days when we were unhappy, we understood that we needed someone else to set us in the right direction.

High school was different; we had men and women as teachers. They were younger, more sophisticated and modern. Sometimes I liked the teacher and sometimes not, it depended on their personality and the subject they taught. The subject that I enjoyed the most was Italian poetry, with poems from Giovanni Pascoli and Gabriele D'Annunzio. I also liked Latin with its rhetoric—rosa, rosarum, rosas, etc. etc. Geography was not my favorite—I could never remember: was it north or south? And I had a hard time remembering—if the sun went around the earth or the earth went around the sun. I enjoyed social studies. It was more interesting—maybe because I would learn what happened in ancient times—especially the Roman years with Cesare and Messalina.

I took many different classes in high school. I leaned to design, sew and embroider. Even now as a grandmother, I still need to go to school to learn the English language. I am a disaster when it comes to grammar. I still love to have someone near me to teach me much more and to search for the right answer. My most admired "teacher" was the author Leonardo Sciascia, a very cultured and modest man. When he was asked who he was, he answered that "he was a simple teacher". But in reality, he was a great literary man.

1.16. MY NEIGHBORS.

I had many kind neighbors. Most were wealthy farmers. We thought we were too. The street was on the hill, tiny, with no sidewalks. Each family owned their own house. They had a few rooms and one bathroom. It didn't matter how many people lived there. Almost all the houses had a balcony. It was most important to own a house and have a balcony or veranda for the plants, and to communicate with the neighbors. The street was narrow, and there was a bamboo cane (not too long) so we could exchange food with the people across the street.

My mother preferred privacy to frequent visits, but she would always say good morning. She suffered from migraines and wanted it to be quiet. I never saw my parents go next door for conversation, but we talked all the time from the balcony. Every morning we would start early watering all the plants. We had many flowers and aromatic herbs.

As soon as we said good morning, we would start to communicate the news that people had just heard. In the meantime, someone from inside might want to know more. Little by little, we would communicate news from three or four balconies over. This was before television existed. We had our own way to give and receive news. Certainly not everything that was said was the truth. Each person had his own version and would add more good or bad details, depending on whether the person in question was well-liked or not.

2

Life in the States

2.1. AMERICAN DREAM.

Everything happened very fast. It was a very hot afternoon in August. Our house was above the Mediterranean Sea facing Africa. We were sitting in the shade and feeling a breeze. And that afternoon, an old priest named Padre Catanzaro, who had emigrated to America, walked by and recognized my boyfriend, Alfonso. He was there for the holiday of *la Madonna del Soccorso*, which is celebrated twice a year, on February 2nd and August 15th. He stopped and started to talk to Alfonso.

Alfonso spoke of his tailor shop with its five employees. Padre Catanzaro explained about America and the need for good tailors. He asked Alfonso if he would move to America. Alfonso asked him if he was serious. He said, "Padre Catanzaro, you asked me something I have dreamed of all of my life, for such a long time. Did I hear what you asked me right?" The priest said, "In America they need a tailor like you, *tu fai fortuna in America* (you will make your fortune in America)." This was Alfonso's dream. He hugged the priest and accepted his offer.

In Italy it was not easy to be a tailor. In fact, it took a long time to make a suit or a dress by hand. It was difficult to have people pay for the service provided. We knew many clients as friends, as well as many relatives, who came to us for years.

That evening my boyfriend came to my home and asked me to marry him and go to America. I gladly responded, "yes". I did not think much about it. My mother, seeing me happy and carefree, asked me if I was sure I wanted to marry and leave Italy. I had never left our country before. I told her I wanted to do it. She worried for me, having to make such a big decision so fast. She worried about how we were going to do in America, a nation so far away, and not even talking English. But did we think so wisely? But then I said, "*Mamma, non ti preoccupare. Siamo contenti* (mamma, don't worry. We are happy), and she was happy for us. In that special moment, I grew up and felt that I was more mature. This was the first time in my life I had made a decision by myself.

On September 16th, 1961 we got married in the church. A reception followed. My father was unable to walk me down the altar. He had flown to America a few months before with a tourist visa to look for a better life and to have security in his senior years. I deeply missed him. My brother brought me down the aisle with all the love and care he could. On our honeymoon we visited the "Continent" (European travel) for three weeks. We Sicilians were used to our little peninsula and it was wonderful.

When we returned we signed a contract that would send my husband to work in New York. The company was called Witty Brothers. It was located on Fifth Avenue, in New York City. At this time, tailors were very well respected. They were represented by the Amalgamated Union (it was directed by the president, Mr. Patoski, and the Vice President was our *paisanu*, from the same town, Mr. Augusto Bellanca.)

On December 13th, 1961 we left Naples on the *Cristoforo Colombo* ship. We had both been dreaming about America for a long time now. When the boat set sail I could not look back at my family. I felt like I was betraying them. I was leaving my home, my family. The one thing that hurt me the most was the noise of the siren horn while the boat was leaving the Italian land. At that moment many people were weeping, and when I saw that, I thought of my mother and my loved ones.

We went into our cabin that was down many floors, near the machinery. We hugged one another, crying for a long time. We realized that we had really left. We were alone now.

The sailors started singing *Addio mia Bella Napoli, mai piu ti rivedrò* (Farewell my beautiful Naples, I'll never see you again). The passengers on the boat started to join in vocally. In the beginning I was unable to sing because of my deep emotion, but slowly, moments later, I was able to join in. I thought of the Domenico Modugno song *Ritornerò, se Dio vorrà* (If God wants, I will come back). I think that song was written for me.

In the beginning, I was feeling that the trip was not for me. Later on I got used to it. I became friends with many passengers on the boat; also the workers on that boat, who were young Italians. There was a young gentleman, whose name I don't remember, who spoiled us with delicious food.

He knew that we had just gotten married. I believe that this was the reason for his gratitude and affection. He told us that he had been in love with a woman in his town and they wanted to get married. The woman's parents did not like him very much, because he was a sailor. She then married someone else who was living in America. She was traveling on our boat which was taking her to her husband in America. What a story!"

Many stories were shared on the trip, also the birth of a baby, which everyone celebrated. The next day they named him Cristoforo, after the boat. His Godfather, the "Captain" of the boat, baptized the baby. My husband told me that it would be just right, if I had got pregnant, in that case we could have named the baby Cristoforo, too. I didn't like the idea. I wanted my children to be born in America, and that dream soon came true.

The boat shook because of the ocean wind. The cabin was small and had no window. The beds were one up and one down. The old carpet smelled of unknown scents and the bed smelled moldy. The motors were noisy and the smell of the fuel was strong. After a few days, we lost our appetite. I don't think they had the air conditioning on, or if they did it was very low. At lunch and dinner they would ring the bell, but not many people showed up in the dining room—almost all of us were seasick. Finally, on the last evening, there was a farewell party. Each person exchanged addresses, and they ranged from Philadelphia, and Boston, to New York, and other places.

That night no one went to sleep. We knew that we would see American land early in the morning. We went out on the cold, dark deck, looking for a peek at the land like Christopher Columbus did. While I was there, I thought of my relatives that had been living in America for many years. At the time they came to America they had very terrible living conditions on the ship. It was not like our trip. On that one, there were separate places for men only, and women with children, and since there was such poor hygiene, many became ill. Once they arrived at Ellis Island they had to be checked by a doctor. If they were sick they were sent back to their country or were required to spend at least forty days in the hospital in quarantine.

We spent many more hours on the deck waiting for the Statue of Liberty to come into view. It was early in the morning of December 21st, 1961. One passenger had binoculars, but for many hours he only saw water. We wore fine coats, and shoes made in Italy. The coats were very elegant. They were made by Alfonso. Alfonso wore an Alpaca wool coat, blue in color, with two side vents, and a belt (almost like a rain-coat style). I wore a dark gray Alpaca wool coat with a fur collar. It was getting very cold so we went inside to drink some American coffee and get warm. I had never tasted it before then, but in those circumstances it tasted very good.

While I was drinking, Alfonso stayed and watched, and he saw it. Taking advantage of the kindness of Italian men, who were outside, we were able to get to the front. Alfonso and I had a clear view. A passenger started saying "Terra, terra, land, land!" We could not see anything at that moment, even though it was sunrise. Suddenly it was possible to see light, but what was it? We found out that it was the light of the Statue of Liberty. When we got close to it I could not believe that a statue so beautiful existed. It was very majestic, with her raised arm, and it seemed to tell us, "I am here, and I am waiting for you."

It was December 21st, 1961, Pier 42, New York, 12:00 pm. Alfonso and I hugged each other, because our dream had come true—we were together at last in America. I had never felt alone even at that time. We did not know a lot of English. That morning we thought everything was possible. We felt that we were already American citizens. On our landing we found Padre Catanzaro who helped us with the customs processing. And finally I met up with my father. What joy! He had arrived there seven months before. He was looking for a job. We left right away for Brooklyn in a black Cadillac, which seemed to us like a bus. it was so big and spacious!!! We took a tunnel. My uncle Nino told us we were below the level of the water. I became very scared and squeezed Alfonso's hand.

Meanwhile my relatives asked us questions about Italy and Sicily. It was Christmastime, and during the evening we took a walk and enjoyed seeing all the lights and the Nativity scenes. We thought we were in heaven.

Once we arrived home, we found all my father's cousins with their children. I knew a few of them. I'd met them some years before and I was happy to see them again.

We had a delicious dinner with our relatives and their friends. We had spaghetti with meatballs. There were other types of Italian food on the table. I remember thinking, "Will it always be like today" or is this because they are celebrating our coming? I did not expect to witness the use of home made Italian food in America. The concept I had was that the food was commercially prepared in cans, jars and plastic containers.

My father had rented an apartment at 6904–18th Avenue, Brooklyn, New York. It was on the second floor above a store. When we opened the door, there was a wood staircase and a bulb, which was the light. We felt very disappointed…This was not the house I had seen in my American movies!!! The steps squeaked…and the floors. My aunt had put an old Persian rug in to improve the aspect of the place. We thought about the marble tiles in our home in Sicily.

The window faced the back yard. There was a small kitchen, a bedroom and a living room, at that time called a parlor. They were furnished with dark oak furniture. Today maybe it is worth a lot, but at that time I didn't like it. I was disappointed. I expected something new and modern, and I found that!

We stayed in Brooklyn. We spent our first Christmas with my father and our relatives. They lived in a beautiful home on 82nd Street and 12th Avenue, Brooklyn. They lived in Brooklyn after so many years living in New York City. They worked hard and now they were in Brooklyn for a better life.

I have wonderful memories of that Christmas—we had a great dinner. My two aunts cooked so many Italian foods. All their children and grandchildren were there. The used a long, large table they put in the basement (they called it the cellar). I was so surprised and happy to see them celebrate the holiday like we did in Italy. I was thinking maybe in America they would eat at a restaurant, and maybe they would forget the Italian traditions. Instead, they were more interested in celebrating than us in Sicily. They are very attached to their home roots and teaching their children how to behave as if they are living in Sicily in the 1920's or before. I received a black puppy with a red ribbon around his neck. It was not a real dog, but I loved him, and I spoke to him every day when I dusted him. In the beginning I had another companion, a plant. I spoke to it every day, and knew it was alive and I was able to communicate with it.

Alfonso brought home another plant for my birthday and anniversary. We celebrated our first Valentine's Day in Brooklyn, something we never did in Italy. When he came home with a beautiful red box of chocolates shaped as a heart, I was in heaven. I kept the box for many years because I really cherished it almost more than the chocolate. I still love fancy boxes and I save all of them.

In the beginning Alfonso was forced to work in a factory. He would rise at 5:00 in the morning because he had to take the train to his work as a tailor. He learned that the work *sarto* (tailor) did not have any meaning in America. In fact, in clothes factories people worked with Singer electric machines, and other only had the special machine. Alfonso remembered his tailor shop in Sicily and the suits made by hand.

He was able to enjoy lunch and start again in the afternoon. He closed his shop at 8:00 in the evening. In New York, he did not know how to use these machines. He had to begin to do stitching…American style. He sewed pieces of fabric that was going from one machine to another, finally becoming a jacket of low quality. Little by little, he mastered the American way. It was not so easy for a good tailor to sew stitch by stitch by hand, measure, fit, and make the right alterations. Now all at once he had to rush and do fast cheap work, not involving hand work. He had to almost finish the jacket, and then hand stitch and press it. At first he didn't have the time even to control the stitch, but soon he learned.

He was able to finish when everybody else did. He would count the number of pieces made during the day and know the dollars he had earned. He did not need a calculator. He is very sharp in numbers and never used one before or after, as he his favorite subject was mathematics (and geography).

After Christmas, I went to Macys in New York City—there I felt as if I were Alice in Wonderland!!!

January, 1962. New York became colder. This was something new for me, because we never had snow in Sicily. It snowed so much that nobody was able to go to work. I was waiting for the holiday to run its course and then we would look for jobs. It was joyous. The Sunday after Christmas we went to see a New York Radio City Christmas Show, with the Rockettes. It was a wonderful show. For a week I kept seeing the dancers, the characters of the Nativity, and the beautiful tree in front of my eyes.

At the end of January, my Aunt Caterina brought me to the factory at 38th Street, between 7th and 8th Avenue, New York, on the 8th floor, where she worked. We started at 71st Street Station and arrived at 34th Street Station, New York. Most of the people were Italian. They made elegant cocktail dresses. They gave me one to put the finishing touches on. I felt confident because I thought I knew how to do it. The problem was that I was not familiar with an electric machine. I was used to a pedal machine. I started…and I almost broke the needle. They explained to me that this machine was very fast and delicate, and I learned to be so fast, fast, fast. One day, after many years work, I caught my finger in the machine. The needle went into my thumb and cut it in a few pieces. They took me to the hospital, where the doctor put me to sleep, took off the fingernail, and took out the needle, which was in two pieces. For a few weeks, the pain was bad. It was painful having my nail missing. When I returned to the shop, all the girls said that now I was a really experienced operator. They said that almost every one had that experience. Now we know what "fast machine" meant.

I did have problems making conversation with people. Almost all spoke English, but because some of them knew Italian I could talk to them or my aunt translated for me.

We rode the train. My aunt bought an American paper (tt that time, people did not want to be recognized as non-English speaking immigrants). I did not understand a word of it, but I looked at the pictures. Here was a photo of Liz Taylor in Rome to act in the movie, "Cleopatra." The paper wrote her love story with Richard Burton.

In March, I joined an evening class to learn English. My teacher was an old Italian man, born in the U.S.A. He taught me small amounts of English. Reading was very hard for me—I tried with enthusiasm to speeeeeak my broooooken Englishhhh.

My father left for Italy. After a few months, I felt very lonely. The relatives I called Aunt and Uncle were very good to us, but I missed my own family. We wanted to start a family of our own. The desire for a baby became strong. Fortunately in June I found out I was pregnant (a few friends even suggested that I had better working for a few months first, make money, and then have a baby)

The news of the pregnancy made us very, very happy. We were going to have some company. We were not alone anymore. In the first months I didn't say anything to anybody—I told no one I was expecting. In the third month, I was riding the train with my aunt. When the train was in the gallery of Canal Street I felt so hot and dry. I felt faint. I was standing up near my aunt and no one offered me a seat, but before that, I felt sick. My aunt was nervous and confused, and asked me, "Are you pregnant?"

They tried to open my heavy dress to give me relief. Already we had reached the 40th street station in our daily ride. Well, that day everybody knew the good news. Before that, my aunt was worried, but after that she was happy for me. She knew we wanted a baby. She was also happy because she never had any children, and now she felt like she would have a grandchild.

The months of pregnancy were not so easy. I felt queasy, especially when I traveled. So my aunt tried always to find a seat for me. I worked until December. The doctor told me to stop after Christmas, and I did. I was fat already and my baby moved so much, like he wanted to come out. The test to tell whether it was a boy or girl didn't exist then so we didn't know. For a couple of months I stayed home. The doctor said everything was okay. My husband couldn't wait to have the baby. He was hoping for a son. Every night he asked me what week I was in, and how many days more?

In Monday morning, March 18, at 6 a.m., after my husband had already left for work, I felt the pains start to come. I called my cousin. My husband was far away at work. My cousin came quickly and brought me to Carson C. Peck Memorial Hospital in Brooklyn, NY. The birth was natural with12 hours of labor.

On March 18, 1963, at 6 PM, ANTHONY WAS BORN!!! What a joy! My family had grown to three. My husband came at night with a beautiful flower, happy for having a son.

We had a new little bassinet. While I was pregnant I had covered it with white lace, doing all the stitching by hand because we did not have a sewing machine. I covered the ruffle with blue ribbons and put the bassinet by our bed.

We bought a washing machine. I didn't need it before. I washed everything by hand. After washing the diapers, I boiled them by pouring in the hot water to disinfect them. We didn't have a dryer yet, so the diapers were dried on the hot radiators every night.

Another big job at night was to prepare the formula. I boiled the bottles for a few minutes in a special container that had a plastic rack that held the bottles upside down. In the meantime, I diluted the powdered milk with hot boiled water, and after the bottles were cooled down, I filled them with 6 or 8 ounces of formula and saved them in the refrigerator to use the next day. For supper I gave him the star shaped *pastina* (tiny pasta) and for meat we used the little baby jars. I felt very lucky for not having to prepare the meat and vegetables. The most he loved to eat was beef and vegetables, and carrots.

I remained home with joy to raise my son. My husband thought it was better for the child to have his mother with him every day. I was happy to stay home and take care of my baby. I missed my mother even more than before. I was upset that he could not know his grandparents. We phoned once or twice a year. At that time it was expensive to telephone to Italy, and we had only one salary. We made some sacrifices, but the baby had the best of everything, especially the fine wool clothes from Italy and the fine leather shoes.

We still lived in the 18th Avenue apartment. For fun we watched the TV. On weekends our favorite programs were Lawrence Welk, Bonanza and The Ed Sullivan Show. We had an old brown wood cabinet TV. It was square with two doors that open and close like a china closet. The picture was small, 13 inches, black and white.

Anthony was a strong and beautiful baby. Naturally we wanted another one. Fifteen months later, July 3, 1964, VINCENT WAS

BORN!!! What joy. We have another son, and our family numbered four.

When I knew Vincent was about to be born, my husband again had just left for work. I called my cousin again, and left my baby with my mother. She had come a few months before with my dad to help me with the baby. I was more content to have some help. We had a sofa bed, and they slept in the living room. The birth was natural and easier than before (3 hours labor, thank God). We bought another crib for Anthony, and put the bassinet on the other side of our bed. We felt so rich and happy to have two babies near us.

For four months we stayed there and then Alfonso was able to find a second, better job and we rented a new larger apartment. Our boys had their own furniture and their own room. Every morning the milk man delivered the milk. He left two bottles in an aluminum container near the door on 18th Avenue, Brooklyn.

Alfonso worked in a factory during the day and his new job was in another place from 6:00 to 9:00 in the evening. He put the finishing touches on men's custom made suits. He asked me many times to keep the baby awake, but it was not always possible. The children were growing up and we missed the presence of our family.

On July 1, 1966, two days before Vincent was two years old, for his birthday we flew in a plane, an Alitalia 747 jumbo jet for the first time. It was the year this big plane from New York could fly for 9 hours. We stopped in Rome for a couple of days to see my husband's family.

After Rome we took another plane and arrived in Sicily! Finally we could hug our families who were meeting our children for the first time. What a joy! Two weeks later my husband came back to the U.S.A. The children and I stayed for an extra three weeks. What a trip! We went to the beach and to the mountains. We had a wonderful time. Sadly, the farm was not the same anymore. My paternal grandmother, my *nonna*, was not there anymore. She had died two years before, just as my son was christened. My mother told me later so that I would not get the bad news too soon. She knew how upset I would be.

Going to the farm and not seeing her with her arms open was really devastating for us. I had imagined many times she wanted to see me running to meet her again. She couldn't write to me, and no one ever did it for her. All the time my family said she was happy to know she was going to be a great-grandmother again, but she never saw me anymore or my babies ever. I took flowers to the cemetery, but seeing her picture made me sad. Thank God, I at least had that time. Both of my maternal grandparents were happy to see their American grandchildren.

Coming back to Brooklyn, we started our life again. The *nostalgia* did not leave us, but actually became stronger. In the meantime, after 5 years, we received our American Citizenship.

2.2. ITALIAN CITIZEN AGAIN.

After living in the United States for 5 years and having children born here, it was right for me to become an American citizen. It would give me the right to vote. I felt that it was my duty to think for the future of my children and vote, hopefully for the right person.

But to become an American citizen I would have to renounce my Italian citizenship. I felt that I was a traitor to my lovely Italy. I tried to convince myself that it was just on paper—that I was still an Italian. I thought that one day when my husband and I retired, we might go back to live in Italy and once again become Italian citizens. But instead, one day I read in *America Oggi* (America Today) that thanks to the President and a new law, I could again become an Italian citizen and not lose my American citizenship. The next day I ran to the Italian Consulate to revive the Italian part of my life which I had lost for some time. With dual citizenship, a great law, I would have the oxygen to live as a proud Italian-American Citizen.

On July 12, 1972 we left the U.S.A. after 10 years to live in Italy. We rode on the Raffaello boat because we had so many sentimental things to take with us. It was summertime and the ride was better—the seas were calm. On the boat we spent beautiful days and nights. My husband made tuxedos for our young sons and they looked adorable in them.

We settled in Rome, Via Valsolda 149 (Montesacro). We stayed with my husband's family. Our children went to the Catholic school, but they had a problem with the language. They knew a dialect, not the Italian. In the beginning my husband was happy with his shop (he opened a tailor shop). After a while we started to miss America, and were very confused. We were called *gli Americani*. I realized…in the U.S.A, we were "The Italians" and here we are "The Americans." I felt like a stranger in my land that I had strongly missed. Finally I understood that I did not belong here anymore!!!!!

We decided to return back to the U.S.A. How could we tell our families? When I told my mother, she asked me, "What is happening? You cried so much because you wanted to return to Italy and now you want to leave again?" But she was happy we returned to America, especially since my dad knew that in the U.S.A we could have a better future for our children. I love America.

Sometimes I still feel a deeply torn. Italy and America are like my two eyes. Both of them are precious and needed. I feel like a person with two hearts. I felt as if I had two mother countries, one Italian and one American. The natural one in Italy and the adoptive one in the U.S.A. The one which was my first had taught me how to live in a new country. I thought I had left my home there which was built out of many sacrifices.

In the beginning, life in America had been very hard, but I feel more American than Italian now. We had problems getting along in Italy, even with relatives. We didn't feel as close anymore.

We came back to the U.S.A. after nine months. We explained to our families, and cried that even though we were born in Italy, our life was not there anymore. My children and I flew back by plane, and my husband left by the Michelangelo ship.

The situation was different now. We had added two children, and we had no house and no job. Now we were more responsible. We were not the same careless young people discovering the new land. Now we know what to expect and the sacrifices we must make to start our American Dream again.

America always welcomed people with open arms. Especially our "Statue of Liberty" was there again waiting for us. For two weeks my children and I stayed at my aunt's house. She was happy to see us back and welcomed us with open arms. Soon I rented four rooms on 84th Street, Brooklyn, enrolled the children in school and started again. My husband got back and returned to work at his old job, and in the night started a designer course. The children started their classes and they were happy. We both worked, and after a couple of years we were able to buy an old house. We fixed the first floor and opened a small tailor shop that was open at night.

We put the finishing touches on peoples' clothes after working in the factory all day. We learned to drive and bought an old Ford Maverick (it was a lemon.)

Our children were growing up well, and helped us in the shop, but the neighbors next door had wise guy kids. Two years after we moved in, after we had the house almost fixed and settled, the house next to ours (attached to ours) caught on fire, which set fire to our home.

It was 9 p.m. when the flames started to come into our apartment on the third floor. We escaped the fire, and in that moment we were glad our family and our dog Luck were safe and sound, but we lost almost everything. My cousin brought us into his home and I spent all that night crying.

We gave the dog to another cousin who lived in Long Island. He took the dog with him to the pizzeria where he worked and somebody took him. We never saw him again. My sons were devastated that they would never see him again. They missed him but we did not have a choice to bring the dog into somebody's house. We are thankful that he helped us humans.

After a couple of days we rented a small apartment on Staten Island (20, Nome Avenue). This was going to be the third time we had settled down!!! After a few months we bought our first new car, a rust colored Buick Skylark.

I believed in miracles, with love and unity. In our family we would survive this misfortune. By now, our children were teenagers and in good health. They went to school and had part-time jobs. My husband and I were working hard and saving money. He worked for Bergdoff-Goodman in New York as a fitter in the Men's Department for 10 years. Certainly, we had to start again. We were already looking for our third American dream.

In two years, we bought a small new beautiful house. My children grew up as hard-working and respectful sons. They attended the Port Richmond High School. I planted my own flower and vegetable garden. We bought new furniture. For a few years we had a new dog. My son Vinny found this puppy in a mechanic shop where he worked part time. He brought him home before we had the new home. He called him Joel. We started to have better luck when we started our life in this house. We worked very hard, but we were more content.

Still the desire to be near my Italian family was strong. I missed them and it was hard with no parents, no siblings.

Italy became a place where we spent our beautiful vacations. We go back to Italy every couple of years and we witnessed how Italy was changing. It was becoming more modern, mirroring the U.S.A. in TV shows, soap operas, movies and children's names. When we were children, people named their children after their grandparents, and they were many "Marias" and "Giuseppes". Now we hear Gessica, Giusi. In U.S.A. Italian is very popular. Restaurants and stores have Italian goods, even if the owners are Jewish or Asians.

Young people who speak Italian are very proud of it. I know that about 40 years ago we were considered ignorant. Now we were finally appreciated!!! Now we have Italian professional people in politics. There are brilliant men, sons of Italian immigrants, who are in government. Like Judge Antonin Scalia, Governor Mario Cuomo, Mayor Rudolph Giuliani. I hope one day there will be an Italian-American President of the United States of America.

I didn't even believe in politicians when I arrived in America. The United States President was John Kennedy. All America was in love with him and Jacqueline, his wife. The citizens admired everything they did. I remember the sad day we lost him. I was in New York with my son in my arms when I heard that terrible news. I felt my arms lost their strength. It was unforgettable, tragic news.

The other brother, Robert Kennedy, his death was another tragedy. Then there was the loss of the good person and black leader, Martin Luther King, Jr. It was so terrible with one tragedy following another in those years. Then came the Nixon time. That was the first time I voted after I became an American citizen. I was glad to vote and do my duty, and I voted for Nixon for my leader. I was so disappointed to hear of the Watergate scandal, I started to feel politically insecure. I felt that there were not so many honest people, and that the politicians didn't deserve the power they had.

2.3. MY LIFE IN AMERICA.

I have spoken, narrated and written of everyone and everything—and America? This is great, generous second "home" country that is always ready to "Welcome All". Many things are said of "Her": Capitalist, Liberal—a "Minestrone of races and colors, wise men and ignorant, multi-billionaires and homeless live in harmony.

Many families have been "broken up" by coming to America—but America has enriched them—using their intelligence and their industrious hands, with their sweat and after many tears and sacrifices, they finally realized there ideal—the American dream.

From the first moment of anger or nostalgia or hate, we say we will leave her—but we never do—or if we do we return. She is a grand passionate lady; always there with her arm raised up to signal us that she is waiting for us. She is always ready to embrace us and hug us. She loves us and now we also love her.

Yes indeed, we love this beautiful nation which adopted us with unconditional love and generosity. More than forty years have passed since we came to the U.S.A., forty three, precisely.

Forty-three? And how old am I? I look at the calendar. It is April 19th and in two days it is my birthday. Actually it is one day to my real birthday. My mother said, "You were born on April 20th, but we declared you the next day because it was a holiday (the birth of Roma) so it was a famous event." The problem is not one day before or after. My dilemma is: am I an Aries or Taurus? I declare like my birth certificate said, April 21, 1938—Taurus.

I turned 66 years young. Young they said; I don't think so. The mirror doesn't lie. Time passes and our body shows its age. I still feel young in my mind, in my lifestyle. In my thoughts I try to be young too. To sum up, I do not want to go back to my youth—it passed a long time ago—my first twenty years in Italy.

I remember the war bombardment. When the siren would sound we all had to go to an underground cave. I remember the American soldiers coming into Sicily—especially the chewing gum. I was too young to know exactly what this meant, what kind of life this was. That important group of politicians in the Italian cabinet changed Italy and gave it a better life style.

Still, when we were young we were not happy with what we had. We wanted to try a different life style and hope for better. America was not really what we expected. In the beginning we were so disappointed. The life was harder than in Italy. We didn't understand the language or the culture. We were so young and inexperienced. We thought we would find things easy like people said," The streets are paved in gold. Instead, the work was harder than ours, and took more hours. We thought we were experienced with sewing machines. Instead, we did not know a thing about the electric machine. We thought we knew America because of the American films, but the reality was different.

It was not easy for two young people to adjust alone. We tried to stay. We tried to live. Finally, at last we understood that our family began and grew in America and we were happy to stay. My forty years in America passed so fast, I cannot believe it is really over.

Anyway, to sum up, I spent the first year busily discovering America. It was just Brooklyn and New York City, but for me, I traveled all of America. The second and third year were the best years of my life. I became a mother of two sons. The years since I have been busy and happy to take care of my children, my husband, the housework.

I was never completely happy. I felt the distance of my family in Italy. I thought of them every day. Thanks to the birth of my sons, the days passed quickly. Before I knew the time had passed my son was already starting to go to kindergarten. Then I was even busier as I had to run to the school every morning, and for a year I stayed home with my younger son. The next year, they were both in school and not babies any more, but good-looking young men. After I took them to school I had a part time job as a dressmaker near the school until three o-clock. Then I would stop, pick up the boys at school, and go home. We had a busy day together: school, homework—sometimes we went to the nearby park.

No one taught me to be a mother. I had nobody near me, mother or sister, to tell me what to do. I learned day by day by my self through experience. So many times when my children cried, I cried with them because I did not know what I was to do. There was an Italian pharmacy across the street from my home. There were two Italian-American brothers there that spoke a little Italian. Whenever I had a problem or the boys got hurt, I ran to them for some help.

They were so good to me. They told me their mother was Italian too, and never spoke good English. They read all my important documents and were our counselors. They explained so many things about how to take care of my sons. I tried to be a good mother (I hope so) and I wanted to teach them good manners. After we came back from Italy and lived at 84th Street, they joined the Boy Scouts. They had a nice time playing sports. They loved any kind of sports, but most of the time loved working.

As soon as it was summer and school was closed, they had to find jobs. Sometimes the school teachers found a job for them. One time for parents' open house night I talked with one teacher and I complained that my sons didn't want to study very much, that they were more interested in their jobs. The teacher, Mr. Webber, said to me that not everybody could be a professor. He said they were good boys, and to let them work—one day you will be happy they did. He was right. Both of them are hard-working, honest men. I'm proud to have two sons that are so hard working.

With God's help, they now had their own family, and already I'm a grandmother too.

Mamma mia, am I already a *nonna*? Not too long ago I remember I was an Italian teenager with my face full of freckles. Every night we used a stinging white cream on them. That was the cosmetic my sister used. That was the time I was in a rush to be a teenager—*una signorina*. When we were young we thought that time would never pass.

But the time passed so fast, between good times and bad, between Italy and America. I crossed the ocean many, many times—a few times with the whole family and a few times with my husband. A lot of the time he couldn't come because of his work.

My husband is a hard-working honest man. He has worked for 38 years without stopping. For him, work was the first commandment. He loves his work and puts in it all of the time and attention required, and never shows his nerves.

For a few years, we worked together. I won't say we never fought. On the contrary, like every couple, we had different ideas, and especially when we were young we wanted to fix the world. I wish I understood then what I know now. I tried to be a good wife. We had respect for one another and did our best to help each other.

Now a few years have passed since we both retired. We both try to take it easy. Even now we scream and argue—we each want to do it like Frank Sinatra—"MY WAY". But now we do not have the power, so we sing: "Everything is Beautiful", and "Don't Worry, Be Happy".

We pass the time between grandchildren, family and friends—long-time friends from the time we were in Brooklyn. Our children grew up together. Today one of my sons and his family live in Brooklyn (where he works at a dry cleaners), and my younger son lives with his family in New Jersey and is a custom tailor like his father.

Certainly life is not a beautiful rose garden—even in the most beautiful gardens the wild grass tries to grow all over, so it is the gardener's job to take care, to watch that all the wild grasses do not grow. We need to pull them out before they start to take over. We try—we hope to manicure a perfect, beautiful rose garden.

2.4. MY HUSBAND

My husband is my partner. He is the most faithful friend of my life. He stands by me all of the time with his love and support. With his modesty and goodness, he had the patience to wait for me until I felt love for him. His family came from a town called Valledolmo [near Palermo]. They came to Sciacca to work. His grandfather and his three sons were bricklayer contractors, or to be more exact, Stony Brick Contractors. They worked to strip the rocks from a marble mountain. They would break the stone into big pieces with explosives. Depending on orders from other contractors, they would select different size cuts. This kind of rock is used more for highways, or rural houses. They came to Sciacca to construct the railroad and the tunnel here.

This big contractor took a long time to finish the hard work and finally my city had the train called "La Littorina." It was a train with three or four railroad cars, and it went to all parts of Sicily. With this railroad we were lucky because we did not have to travel any more for uncomfortable hours with a horse and a carriage.

For a long time all of the sons worked with their father on this project. My father-in-law was the oldest son. Thus, he was ready to look for a girl. The old saying was, "Moglie e buoi dei pasei tuoi" (Get your wife and ox from your own hometown). Nevertheless he fell in love with a girl who was a "forestiera" (not from his town). Her family came from a very small town called Favara (near Agrigento) to work in Sciacca, which, in comparison to other smaller towns, was then an industrial city. So many people came here to find a better way of live. In a few months they were married and they built their home and family of three boys and one girl. My husband is the oldest. They are a family of artisans, much different than mine. They had modern ideas and a freer lifestyle.

How did we get married? Maybe love is like electricity. It needs the negative and the positive not to explode!!!

We met when we were very young. He was my younger brother's classmate. I know he was interested in me when I was attending the seventh grade. Every day at the school door I saw him waiting for me in front of the door, and he followed me to the end of the street. This continued for a long time, but I never gave him the opportunity to talk to me. I was not ready for a boyfriend. When the boys looked at me I looked at them too. But I looked more for a friendship than a boyfriend. At that time, a girl was not permitted to have a male friend.

For a few years I stayed boyfriend-free, not saying yes or no to anyone. For a long time he tried to talk get me to go with me, but I did not agree and maybe he got angry, because for a few weeks I did not see him. But because of his love for me, and his patience in overcoming many obstacles, little by little I fell in love with him. Every time I did not see him I missed him. Now I was sure—I loved him. For a few years we saw each other on the sneak in the street with our friends for company. Then we were became engaged and we were lucky to have an opportunity to go to America . Then we were happily married.

Certainly in every marriage everything is not perfect. We had different ideas. He came from a modern family so I expected him to be more liberal. I was from an ancient conservative family but I am more liberated and modern than they are. From love we learned to respect the most important rule: to respect each other's ideas. I think love is not looking in each others eyes, but love is looking in the same direction. Love means to be faithful for life.

2.5. TAILOR.

When I think of a tailor my mind sees an old, patient man wearing big thick glasses, sitting on a wooden stood with a dusty pillow, curved over a sewing machine, and threads of all different colors hanging around him. I think of him carefully stitching garments with little invisible hand stitches. He uses a pedal sewing machine situated in front of a window, with his table full of pins, needles, tape measures, chalk, a big dark scissor and a heavy coal iron.

But that was in the early 1900's. Today, a tailor is a young man, a cultured clothier full of energy, seeking to create new designs and styles for masculine fashions for the well dressed man.

A very elegant hand-made tailored suit is one of the most prestigious items in a man's wardrobe. The process of having a custom suit made begins with choosing the right fabric. His skin tone, shape, height and coloring are all important factors in choosing the right color and material. Usually a tailor will suggest virgin wool or cashmere for the cold winter, and cotton or linen for hot summer days.

The tailor starts to take the measurements, observing the body. Each body has a different posture and each person needs to have his own individual pattern. The material is cut, then basted together with hand stitches. Now it is ready for the first fitting. The most important part of the jacket is the collar. The shoulder line is what gives the jacket all the balance. The man must also choose the right design for his suit. He can choose the pockets (vents in center, sides, or none at all) and the lapel. The final touches are the most important. The sleeves must be the right length making sure to leave them ¼ inch short so as to show off the cuff on the shirt sleeve. For an elegantly finished sleeve, the sleeve should have a hand made working button hole—half inch cut, stitched around with one hundred silk loop stitches to show mother of pearl buttons—always leaving one button open. What a special look that is!

For the pants, the right rise, pockets style, and a comfortable waistband—leave some room for a nice dinner—are always important. A tailor uses plain bottoms for casual pants and cuffs for dressier trousers or an elegant look.

After a couple of weeks of patient fitting and careful stitches, the suit becomes a "work of art", ready to wear proudly, to possess and to really feel "like a million dollar man".

The oldest artisan trade is the tailor. Tailoring in my husband's family is something that comes naturally, in his DNA. His maternal grandmother was so proud to say and she repeated it many times, that their family "had been tailors for seven generations". Her father, almost all of her uncles, aunts, cousins (male and female) were all tailors. Each generation taught the next from the time they were babies. The family occupation was always all of the relatives working together.

In the time of war, his grandmother was not simply a seamstress, but a "tailoress," with all the female members and the very young boys helping. All of the men, like my husband's father, were in the military. The women and children made military uniforms. They finished them and sewed buttons by hand but because there was a shortage of thread, they used the material from the parachutes of the American soldiers to make thread. They would cut long strips of material and pull the thread from the woven texture and roll it like a spool. This was the job of the very young—everyone did something. The thread was brownish in color and very strong—good for tightening the buttons. With the larger remnant pieces they were able to make things for the family.

Alfonso, my husband, was 8 years old at the time and already was learning. He would sew the inside seams with long hand stitches so that the material would not shred, learning to make clean seams like a Merrow machine. In the meantime, he would look for small pieces of material on the floor. He would take them and roll them very tightly in a round form, sew it with small tight stitches and form the small remnants together, making his first soccer ball. Certainly it could not bounce, but it was good for kicking. Because it was war time, no one could afford to by anything but what was necessary, so you can imagine what it was like to have a soccer ball.

My husband grew up going to school and doing his schoolwork and working in his cousin's tailor shop, but his first love was soccer. No matter how hard he worked he always found time to sneak away from the tailor shop to play a game. Alfonso's number was nine and he played "centro avanti" or front center. He was a good player and he was very fast. However, his father did not approve of him playing soccer instead of working. His father forbid him to play during the week, so only on Sunday was he permitted to play.

One week, however, his father was out of town doing work and Alfonso left the tailor shop to go play soccer. His father came home early to find that his son was not at work. This infuriated his father, so he went out to look for him at the field where he played soccer. When Alfonso found out that his father was looking for him, he tried to hide so his father wouldn't find him. His father decided to wait to speak to Alfonso when he came home. Before the family sat down to eat dinner that night, Alfonso's father sat him down and explained to him the importance of hard work and that playing all the time would not put food on the table. He explained that he would have to provide for a family and work was the only way to do so. He also showed Alfonso how good he had it to be working in a house with good people and a comfortable atmosphere.

Alfonso understood what his father was saying and stopped playing soccer and concentrated on work. However, his love for the game never died as he would go to games every Sunday afternoon before coming to see me. I understood to let him go to see his game because he would work hard all week and look forward to going to the games. I would never go with him because it was inappropriate for a woman to go to the games where the men were shouting vulgarities and yelling. My husband now is happy to see that his son can be apart of my grandson's life and play with him and know that it was all because of his hard work and sacrifices.

For a few years, the cousins all worked together in the tailor shop. Once Alfonso became a teenager, he began to dream about having his own tailor shop and accomplishing something all on his own. Alfonso moved to Rome from Sciacca when he was 19 to live on his own and learn more about the tailor trade. He rented a small studio apartment, got a job and enrolled in a tailor school. He worked hard all day, as he needed to pay for his rent and his school and then would go to school after work. Once he finished school and had a diploma, he returned back to Sciacca to open his own business.

He rented a room and with the help of his family, got the business started. He used his family's pedal sewing machine, scissor, mirror, cotton thread spools, a large table, some stools, but most of all he had his new ideas fresh from Rome. I was reminded of the movie "Fiddler on the Roof" the way my husband started his business. By the age of 22, my husband had his own tailor shop, and his dream was starting to come together. He hired a few young men to help him with the work and would work all week. They had a lot of work but there was one problem. People never paid what they owed on time. Sciacca was a small town and every one of his customers was family, a friend or someone he knew from the town. Alfonso would order the suit fabric without a deposit and complete the entire suit and have to wait to get his money back. His employees would deliver the suit to the man and the man would give the boy a tip and tell him he would see Alfonso during the week. He could never go to the customer and ask for the money because they would be insulted. My husband sometimes did not have very much money for himself once he paid his workers and took care of the expenses of the store. He felt that none of his customers appreciated the talent he had and the hard work that he put into each and every suit. His dream was to make money and live a comfortable life. The only place that could truly make this dream come true was America.

Alfonso and I moved to America and we worked very hard for many years. We never complained about it because we always got paid when we were supposed to and we were taught to work hard. We made many sacrifices for many years and then Alfonso went to another school to improve his trade even more. He finally found a good job as the head tailor of a large and expensive department store in Manhattan, Bergdorf Goodman. His impeccable manners, modesty and his determination to please his customers made him very successful. His customers encouraged him to open his own tailor shop. A customer who was in the real estate business found us a small space on the sixth floor of 57 West 57th Street. All of our loyal clients followed us and we became very successful. I even had to go to design school and start to help him. Alfonso had customers such as Anthony Hopkins, Harrison Ford, Kathleen Turner, Elton John, Tony Bennett, and Ann Ziff. Alfonso would create the beautiful custom suits and I would take care of the fine, specially

designed dresses for the women. We are so proud that we lived our
dream and even our children have carried on our dream into their own
dream and also have been successful. Alfonso even went on to be called
"Manhattan's best tailor" by Town and Country Magazine in 1993. He
was known throughout the entire country and I could not be more
proud that my husband worked so hard and accomplished all he
wanted to and it proved that even the most modest tailor can have his
own "kingdom".

2.6. MY CHILDREN.

My children have been the most precious gift life has given to me. Since
the first month I got married, my first thought was that I hoped one
day to become a mother and have my own children.

I loved my parents, my sister, my brothers, and my husband. But
when I became a mother life gave me something really mine that I
loved above the most good and beautiful thing in the world! I feel that
their lives took something of my flesh and blood and they became a
person that was a continuation of myself. I'm so happy to be their
mother and proud of them.

Since they were very young children they were good scholars and
very hard working people. They started to work very young and they
were very responsible. We know they love their spouses and are now
lovely parents of beautiful children.

I thank them so much for passing on to me the indescribable joy of
being a grandmother. It is so beautiful to see my children have their
own children and to pass on my love for them to my grandchildren.
This is the real high point of happiness (thank God).

And thanks to our parents for giving us the life we have today.
Because I believe to have a good life you have to first have good parents

to give you a right direction in life. Thanks to my dear sons I feel more secure while I am getting old, knowing that I can count on them.

I am very proud of my children who speak English and Italian, even a dialect. They can have conversations with relatives and Italian friends. They are good American citizens and very respectful Italian sons. They are happily married to Italian girls, and they are happy parents.

2.7. MY GRANDCHILDREN.

The greatest blessing in the world is having my precious grandchildren. I know that now my heritage, customs and traditions will be carried on with my grandchildren. The first of my six angels from God was my first granddaughter, Bianca. My world changed from a happy mother, to an even happier grandmother. The first time I saw her beautiful little face I could only think of how much she looked like my son, Anthony, especially when she moved her little nose. Our family cherished her beauty. She has grown into a very sensitive, loving little girl.

The second happy event was when my only grandson, Vincent Alfonso, was born. He and Bianca are only 18 days apart which allowed me to have double the joy. We were so proud that we now had Vincent, the only grandson, to carry on our family name.

After three years another beauty was born. Her name was Alexandra, and what a joy to have another little girl. She is caring and full of joy.

The beauty of my family was kept alive with the birth of Gianna, who came to us only one month after Alexandra blessed our lives. She was full of spirit and she was a like a little doll, with red curly hair. I was with my mother in Sciacca when Gianna was born and my son Anthony told me that he had another beautiful daughter. I could not wait to come home and see my fourth grandchild.

After a few years, while I was living in Florida, I received more good news. Both of my daughters-in-law were expecting their third babies. God blessed me to be a grandma two times more. We eagerly expected the pleasant event. My fifth granddaughter is named Sophia. She arrived as beautiful as her sisters and cousin.

Another great gift was given to my family only twenty-nine days later. Her beauty is explained in her name. Isabella was born with the face of an angel. We call her "Bella" for short because in Italian that means beautiful. We completed our family that now counts one dozen. I love all my grandchildren. They make my life complete. We have six beautiful grandchildren! Each one of them is our great joy. We had finally fulfilled our "American dream".

2.8. MY DAUGHTERS-IN-LAW.

I have two wonderful sons. I never tried to have other children, because my sons were born only 15 months apart. My sons grew up full of life and happiness. Time went by quickly and they soon became teenagers and started to bring girls home to meet me and my husband. I was so happy because I felt that one day soon, I would have a "daughter" in my home.

Vincent was the first one to bring home a lovely girl. I could tell right away that they were in love and wanted to get married. I was very happy and loved her from the first day I met her. I was finally going to have a daughter. From the day they were married, Daria called me Mom and my husband Dad—I had a daughter.

My other son, Anthony, was still single. I hoped that he too would find the right girl and that he would be happy. Soon he too brought a young lady into our home, she was just as sweet as Daria and we welcomed her in the same way. Soon my dream of having daughters came true when Anthony married Lisa. I love both of them dearly and although they may never love me as their own mother, we can share a common love for my sons. They know that I love my sons the way their mothers love them and for that we have the utmost respect for each other that we express through love. They are the wives of my sons and I am the mother. I am never jealous of them, but just to see how happy they make my sons and how much they love and cherish my grandchildren makes me love them as my own children.

2.9. MY ITALIAN-AMERICAN RELATIVES.

Before1950, Italy was visited by many tourists from all over the world—but not by many Americans. But in 1950, the Catholic Church celebrated its Holy Year. So many tourists came to Italy. The first stop was Rome to visit the Vatican—St. Peter's Basilica, full of many ancient and magnificent paintings—the Sistine Chapel—the large St. Peter's Square where on Sunday's Pope would give his Papal Blessing to crowds of people.

Thanks to modern airliners travel became much more comfortable and easier. Tourism increased. When people from Sciacca (*Saccensi*) immigrated to America, in the beginning of the 1900's, they lived in Little Italy (New York) on Grand Street. Later they immigrated to other places—the pescatore (sea people) went to Boston, a beautiful seaport, where they continued their work as fishermen. Some opened fish stores or restaurants. They started to organize many Italian clubs and continued their Italian culture and family traditions of the original country.

Those that were farmers, immigrated to Pennsylvania, to Norristown, a small town situated on the top of a hill—similar to our own town. They worked the fields and lived an agricultural life almost the same way they did in Sicily. Their children became more "urbanized" and were more educated and they worked in shops and offices and others even held more important jobs.

Other Sicilians arrived in the 1960's and settled in Brooklyn, NY, where there is a section known as Little Italy. There is even an avenue there named after Christopher Columbus (18th Avenue). There are many Italian clubs also, where mostly the men pass the time of day playing cards (*scopa* and *briscola*) and drink *espresso* coffee, have *cannoli* or any other type of pastry, or even a fruity gelato. There is even the very Sicilian *frutti di matturana* (marzipan, see recipe section) a sugary almond paste delight that is shaped like and that tastes like fruits. Just like in Sciacca, they are incredible in taste and looks—a real culinary work of art.

Every year in this section of Brooklyn, they celebrate the feast of Saint Rosalia. All of the streets are closed and full of *bancarelle* (street carts) where vendors sell sandwiches of sausages and peppers, *pizza, calzone* and delicious *zeppole* (doughnuts) covered with powered sugar. The street is filled with wonderful aromas with people walking around all night, listening to Italian music and greeting *paesane* (friends from the homeland). Other saints are celebrated as well in other parts of the city—each representing a different town. In such a strange land, people still try to remember and express their own traditional feasts.

In October, there is a very important event the parade for Christopher Columbus day. Every club or fraternity contributes with its own town's costumes. Many Italian companies are also represented. There are bands and groups that come from Italy. Each year an Italian American is honored to be the Grand Marshall of the Parade. People love to show their respect to their mother country. Children wave their three-colored flags—green, white and red.

With pride and joy they show that they are proud to be Italian American people. That special day makes us remember that Christopher Columbus discovered a strange new land and gave us the opportunity to see other people's culture—a mixture of the ancient with the modern—complicated and yet very simple—this land of the American Indians.

Who could think that after a few centuries it would become the most important land in the world?

2.10. Maria's longest trip.

America Oggi (America Today)
December 3, 2000

One day Maria Sciortino was reading the *America Oggi* paper and found a little advertisement that said, "Voi fare un salto in Italia gratis?" (Do you want to "jump" over to Italy free?") The newspaper was looking for stories of Italian immigrants. Maria then wrote a letter to *Oggi*. They called her and said that Maria's story was chosen to be part of the documentary which was a trip to Italy called, "Seven Days in Italy."

Maria and Alfonso went to Italy to make the documentary and to look back on their own roots. They met relatives and had a good time. The documentary was aired at the end of February that year in Italy. During that week Maria wrote a diary and sent it back to *Oggi* when she got home. Because she put so much feeling into her writing, the newspaper decided to publish the diary.

She began by asking herself, "Am I an Italian or American? Sometimes living in two different worlds can be very difficult. But by continuing to think about this, is it curiosity or intellect? As time passes, the answer can change. During the last 40 years, we have enjoyed success and have traveled to many places, but we never have forgotten our roots on the other side of the ocean."

Maria's Italian Diary
September, 2000
As I do every morning, I start my day thinking about Italy and buying the American Oggi newspaper. I read it while I drink my coffee or as I travel to work in New York. One Sunday morning I read a little advice:

Vuoi Fare Un Salto In Italia, Gratis? (Do you want to make a leap to Italy, free)? I am always interested when someone talks about Italy. I am always interested in searching more deeply into my roots and looking for people like me. I have been in the USA for 40 years and I still look for things about my own background. Soon after reading this article I wrote my own story in seven pages and sent it to America Oggi. After a few days I received a phone call telling me my letter was chosen for the Italian documentary. When I told Alfonso he was overjoyed to go back to Italy for seven days and rediscover Italy as a tourist, a visit to the place where we were both born in.

October 2000

The Italian television troupe made an appointment to meet me on 18th Avenue in Brooklyn. I thought there was no better place than 18th Avenue. I lived there when I came from Italy on the shop <u>Christopher Columbus</u>. My children were born there. This place is my home sweet home. Whenever I go back there I feel like I am returning to Sicily. In the afternoon we went to New York to visit our tailor shop. This is where my husband makes sartorial works of art. He was so proud to show his wall holding many pictures of celebrities wearing his custom suits. I thought, "Even a modest tailor can have his own *regno* (kingdom)."

October 9, 2000

Today is Christopher Columbus Day. He discovered this generous and beautiful land—America. I am very proud to be Italian so I went to New York. For these reasons I go to the parade every year. Many people see the Italian people with their carton suitcases tied closed with cords, but they don't see that those suitcases were filled with dreams and hopes for their future. Italians are modest people. It is because of their sacrifices and hard work that we have people like Rudolf Giuliani, Mario Cuomo, George Pataki, Lazio and Judge Scalia. Italians have pride and honor, thanks to those people with their carton suitcases.

October 10, 2000
In a few days we will be leaving on our trip. I start to pack my suitcases. I dedicate this trip to my grandchildren: Bianca, Vincent, Alexandra and Gianna. I hope they get to see Italy with their own eyes some day.

October 13, 2000
I run to the beauty parlor, water my plants, and call my children to say goodbye. The Italian crew come with their lights and cameras. It is time for this beautiful "Italian Adventure" to begin. First stop is Milan.

October 15, 2000
Milano Milan Lugano
I was in Lugano before, but today is different. I discovered a different Lugano under the rain and fog. It looks like a veil is covering the face of a beautiful lady. We visit a church and we walk the streets, and we took a boat. This is a beautiful city. Next stop is Venezia.

October 16, 2000
Venezia-Venice
Venice is beautiful and romantic with a lot of art everywhere. We went all around the city, through the narrow streets and dark canals. In Piazza San Marco, I meet my brother and his wife. I feel such emotion to see my family. I feel a tug at my heart again when I am together with my family. Unfortunately, life changes and we separate each time but we remain together with letters and telephone calls. In the afternoon, we go to Murano. We admire a beautiful glass vase but did not buy it

because it was too expensive. The next time we will buy it. In the canal I see a gondola with a gondolier playing music. I suspected it was for us, and it was. What a surprise! We went along the canal in the gondola. This was something I had never experienced, not even on my honeymoon. It was so romantic. The sun was shining, the music played and I felt like I was on my honeymoon. That night we had dinner and went to the casino to play. It was a really nice day.

October 18, 2000
Firenze-Florence
On the bus we exchanged addresses and photos with people. We talked about our families and told stories. We saw the whole city of Firenze, full of art, with monuments like those in Piazza Signoria. And so much culture such as Michelangelo, Galileo and so many others. In the afternoon I saw my other brother and his wife. It was wonderful. With him I am very comfortable. We are so much alike and very attached to each other.

October 19–20, 2000
Napoli Naples
In Napoli the sun really shone just like the Neapolitan song, "O paese do Sole." I found this city to be clean and the people happy. We saw many sites such as the Mount Vesuvio and the Blue Grotto in Capri. We had a nice all-fish dinner at a restaurant that had lots of music.

October 21–22, 2000
Roma
In the "Eternal City" we visited churches, monuments, squares and fountains. We threw some money in the *Fontana di Trevi*. We had a nice and tasty dinner with *opera* singing and romance.

Alfonso met his sister, sister-in-law and other family members. It was a very happy day. The trip was very successful. I want to thank everybody who worked so hard to make it possible. Everyone was very generous. We felt like we were one big family.

October 23, 2000

Today we came back to America. In one way I was sad and in another way I was happy. I had been in Italy before to visit my family but this time I was a tourist. I saw Italy with different eyes. Every time I go back to Italy, I see more and more Americanization, especially in younger people. I think Italy and America *si vengono incontro* (they reach out for each other; they want to be more like each other). The Americans discovered and love everything Mediterranean, all the food and spices and fashion. American is getting more and more Italian style.

I am happy to see this change. I respect the young people's opinion and ideas. The young are tomorrow's world. There are times when I wonder which is better: the way things were before, or the way they are now. I become sad when I think of how things were in the past when I was young, but I do not want to go back. I want to go forward. I want to look ahead. At times I wonder to myself, "Am I Italian or American?" It is confusing sometimes. I try to stay attached to my Italian roots but in America I became a woman and a mother. I really matured in another culture. I love America as much as I love my right eye, Italy like my left. Both are precious and indispensable. My children and grandchildren were born in America. To have experienced both cultures so intensely as a part of me is wonderful and special. I feel it gives my life a magical touch. I don't think I will ever know the answer to my own question, but it doesn't matter. It is still beautiful to live between Italy and America. They both possess an equal place in my heart.

DECEMBER 31–10:00 P.M.

In two hours the year 2001 will be finished. Our 40th anniversary of arrival to the USA was this month, December 21, 2001. While I am writing, Sara Brightman is singing "Memory." She helps me remember the good and the bad of these forty years of our life between Italy and America. What is left of my family, my land, my people, is a single trunk of belongings.

I am happy to have landed in America, blessed by God with abundance and freedom. I became the mother of two sons, and they gave me the strength to think that we are no longer alone in this strange land. Now I have my American sons. They cheered up my family and enlivened my home. So many years have passed—it was not so easy. Now I am remembering, and as I look back over the 40 years, the first good thought is: My family counts 12 people. This is the blessed gift God gave us for our 40th anniversary.

The year 2001 was one of the most unfortunate for America, the horrible September 11th, remembered by all the American people as the most unforgettable, terrible, sorrowful day.

My husband and I were traveling by bus going from New Jersey to New York. I had my eyes closed, maybe I was asleep. My husband woke me up, frightened, to look at the Twin Towers building covered with smoke. We were in the curve near the tunnel and we could see that terrible scene across the water. I thought it was a terrible fire, and I saw that the smoke was from a few floors. I wondered what had happened?

A girl in the bus heard on her radio that a plane had crashed there. Then we saw an airplane go near. I thought it was going to bring help. I did not see it hit the tower. The girl screamed and said, "Another plane has hit them." I thought I did not understand. The bus stopped and all the people looked out the windows, terrified. Someone called the bus company and told the bus driver to turn the bus back to New Jersey.

Before we reached a mall nearby we knew so many other terrible things happened. My thoughts went to my son, Vincent, who worked in downtown Manhattan. Was he near there? Where was he? I thought about Anthony also. That day I knew he was off work—thank God. I tried to call them, but all the lines were busy or disconnected. So I kept trying to get some answer. Finally I got through and Vincent said, "Mamma, I'm okay."

His office was so near to the disaster that at the first crash he ran and left New York before the tunnel was closed, like a miracle. With his guardian angel at his side, my son made it home. Then I called and talked to Anthony too. I thank God from the bottom of my heart that my children were okay.

My thoughts then went to all the people who were inside the towers when they collapsed. This was most painful. I realized so many people were there—what was happening to them? Before the night we knew that our dear friends' son was missing. He was a fireman, and went there to help the people, and instead remained there in that horrible crash. He was a young father and the loss was painful. We knew a few more people involved with tragedy.

In that week also it was our 40th wedding anniversary. Our sons had planned a surprise party for us. We decided not to do it in that painful time. So many people cried, we did not feel like celebrating. On the following Sunday, our sons, daughters-in-law and grandchildren came home to have dinner together to thank God and celebrate that we were all together *sani e salvi* (safe and sound).

2.11. NAPLES, FLORIDA.

This is a little corner of paradise, situated on the west side of Florida in the Mexican Gulf, is a place called Naples, Florida. The beach is calm, and a beautiful green color. The place is situated on a low tide part of the water. Almost every day you can see a couple of dolphins play in the water. The sand on the beach is as fine a pure sugar and full of many exotic shells. There are so many tropical trees. In the afternoon, you can see the sun go down, and what a beautiful sight that it. All of the clouds change a different color; the sea and sky become to look like one in the horizon. They wait for that beautiful hot sun, little by little the sun goes down very slowly like it does not want to leave, and finally it disappears. To me it is the best sun set in the world. Naples streets are very large and clean, with beautiful palm trees. There are so many shopping malls, like the street Tamiani Trial (41), which is a shopping mall strip.

Florida is wonderful for retired people. Now finally people can do things that they did not do in the younger ages. You see people, in their old ages play tennis, golf, biking, kissing their girl friends, etc. On 5th and 3rd street, there is another retirement place, full of boutiques, and many Italian café's. For golf lovers this is the right place. My little condo is situated on one of the gold courses in Florida. Every day I enjoyed the tranquility, like I am at my grandparent's farm in Sciacca. This tranquility gives me a little "pinch" of Sicily, where I spent my childhood. It brings me back to the days when I was my happiest and had no worries.

In Sciacca everything was dry and old and here in America everything is bright and new. This a modern young world, trying to appeal to the young ones. In this land even the person who dies, tries to die with his eyes open to look better. In this crazy world of today you work till you can find a piece of paradise where you can find relaxation and paradise. The old people here say we should come to Naples because we will live much longer, and I hope that they are right!

3

Sicilian food and traditional recipes.

Living in a time when all is necessary and indispensable, we always try to have more and more, even if it means working day and night. Food, as we all know, is necessary to keep a person healthy, but by using too many ingredients and eating larger portions, we lose enjoyment of eating. Food can only retain its natural taste by being enjoyed in a proportioned size. You must give the right amount of "pinch" in each dish. Many people over-do old recipes that were meant to be one way and they change it to have more. Pasta with sauce is now overpowered by the sauce. Pizza with mozzarella has more mozzarella than dough. Over powering the "extras" will make a person under appreciate the true beauty of the dish.

We think that more is better. Portion sizes became disgusting and unappreciated. Let us try to limit ourselves, giving the correct amount to each dish. Only in this way can food retain its natural taste. We use more and more diversity and quantity and perhaps less and less quality.

3.1. MEDITERRANEAN KITCHEN FROM SICILY.

I grew up cooking, or maybe watching my grandmother, my mother or my sister cooking. I didn't know that there existed so many different ways to cook. I never heard of "The Mediterranean Kitchen".

I never saw my family use a recipe to cook. We would cook everyday, using usually whatever was being sold in the market for that season. Every morning we ran to the nearest market to look for the daily food that the farmers had harvested the day before. I was so happy to see the fruits or the vegetables in all different colors, like they came from the rainbow. I loved to choose all the different colors, but I didn't know which ones had which vitamins and calories. I didn't know the rainbow was full of so many essential nutrients.

We tried to prepare something different, everyday. The only food that was the same everyday was pasta. We would only change the condiments. Almost everyday, we would have a simple tomato sauce and on a few cold days we have *minestra*.

Especially in the winter time, on a cold day we tried to cook with many colorful vegetables. A small amount of money and little bit of time allowed us to arrange hot *minestra* and make the family happy and fill their stomachs with nutritious food. Because Sicily is full of sun and warm weather it helps to produce the right fruit and vegetables and have the real Mediterranean taste.

3.2.1. Summertime breakfast

During the summer, since there was no school, I would get up late and wait for Don Vito to pass. He was a small man, who supported his large family by making homemade lemon ice called *granita*. He used a copper bowl full of ice, lemon juice and sugar. Stirring for several minutes it would soon have the taste of *granita*.

At the sound of his whistle, I would run down the stairs with a glass (we did not have plastic cups then). Every one brought their own glass, the largest you could find, hoping he would fill it. He would measure 10 lire worth no matter how large the glass was. I would go upstairs and begin to dip my bread in the *granita*. It became even sweeter as it melted. It left my stomach cool all morning.

When I got older, I did not run down the stairs anymore when I heard his whistle. Instead, from the balcony, I would lower the glass in a basket on a long cord and then pull it up, like a young lady was expected to do.

3.2.2. Winter breakfast

Our breakfast in Sicily was not so important. At sunrise, the aroma of a good *espresso* would awaken us. We had biscotti or a piece of bread, which we would dip in warm milk with two tablespoons of sugar. It became like a sweet soup that warmed us in the winter. We had no radiators so the walls were cold and damp. However, winter was not as cold in Sicily as it is here, some days it was better on the balcony than inside the house.

Antipasto

In my family, we would begin to eat our dinner at one o'clock in the afternoon. Perhaps, this can explain why our breakfast in the winter was not very important. We actually did not have antipasto. No one was permitted to taste anything before the pasta dish because they did not want us to spoil our appetite. Those tasty tidbits such as fresh cheese, dried sausage, olives, salami and mortadella (my favorite) would be eaten as the filling for a tasty roll.

Dinner

Dinner always began with the Sign of the Cross. Each of us would be seated in our own place. When I was young, we would wish our parents a good dinner by saying, "Bless us papa and mamma" and they would respond, "The saints have given their blessing". As time went on customs changed, but we still used our manners from the elders. Today in Italy, everyone is greeted with "Good dinner to all". I think it must have been very difficult for my father to accept this equality because he was brought up by my grandfather to respect the distance between children and their parents. Parents were not to be treated the same as your school friends, but the people who gave you life. In my father's eyes, elders deserved the utmost respect.

My mother first would serve my father, however if my grandparents or other guest were there, they were served first. There was a great deal of respect, especially for the older people. My brothers were served next, in order of age, then my sister and I. Finally, my mother would serve herself, my humble, sweet, adorable Mother.

Dinner was the occasion for all the family to be together. There was never a time when anyone in my family was late or absent for dinner. It was beautiful to be seated near each other at the little round table, with its beautiful white tablecloth, to eat simple food. A dish of pasta or soup would be followed by a single slice of roasted veal with salad and a half glass of wine.

After dinner, the men would take a nap and my sister and I would clean the dishes. Afterwards, we would close all the windows and leave a small opening to make sure all the flies would get out. Sometimes we would also take a nap or we would sit out on the balcony in the shade to embroider, sew or read a magazine.

Supper
After having eaten dinner, usually at night we preferred something light to eat such as a piece of fish, vegetables or a nice salad (that was what my sister and I preferred). My brothers were satisfied with what we prepared. But often my brothers came in late and they were hungry. My brother would prepare eggs with tomatoes and onions. The aroma would wake us up and one by one we got up and sat with him. We all would eat and talked quietly so that we would not awaken our parents.

3.3. CAKES

3.3.1. *Cubbàita.*

Sicily is full of almond plants. In the first week of February the temperature is still frigid and damp, and it would drizzle most of the days.

The almond plants start to blossom earlier than the others, with the delicate pink flowers and the extraordinary aroma, announcing that spring has come.

This is the first festival Sicily honored: *La Sagra del Mandorlo in fiore* (the Festival of the flowering Almond) and was celebrated in the Agrigento ancient temples. All the nearby farms, with that special blossom, covered the territory with the flowers perfuming the air.

Our farm was full of these marvelous plants. We had an abundant harvest. After the spectacular blossom, then came the almond with a green cover. The new almond had inside a jellylike liquid, sweet to eat. In a few weeks the outside shell dried, and the inside, the almond, started to get hard. Then they are ready. The farmer started to harvest them.

The branches would be pulled down from the tree with a long stick and harvested by hand. They would be brought home and dried more, and then the dried shell would be taken off and the almond with its natural shell would appear. My grandmother would start to roast the almonds and mix with more roasted seeds and fill the baskets, ready to sell.

My mother loved to have this basket full for the holiday cookies, especially for the *cubbàita* (almond nougat) for the special *Immacolata Vergine Maria* festival, December 8th.

At that time she started to prepare it and the apartment started to smell so good. The aroma of caramelized sugar filled all the building. Six families lived in our building (enough), two families on each floor. We lived on the second floor. Every time we cooked something that smelled good, we were almost obligated to bring a little to the neighbors. (It was not nice to have to smell and not taste it.) Every day, the dishes were going up and down, especially if anybody was pregnant. It was really inexcusable not to have the pregnant lady taste everything, so that she wouldn't have a baby with a *disìu* (a birthmark caused by a food desired).

Every time it was my duty to bring the dish, with a few pieces of what was cooking. When going up and down the stairs, I would taste some little pieces, or licked my finger. We were supposed to take some before we ate it. If it was after we ate, it was a leftover, so I would wait and eat after the distributions. The dishes never came back empty. In a few days they would come back full with another specialty.

CUBBAITA

INGREDIENTS

2 pounds almonds

1 pound sugar

2 spoons honey

1 teaspoon cinnamon

Put all the ingredients in a pot with a high flame. Stir constantly with a wood spoon. Let the honey and the sugar melt and caramelize until the almonds become a light brownish color.

Grease a marble counter generously with oil so the mixture will not stick. Pour the mixture on the marble counter and with wet hands keep it together. The mixture is hot. Watch that your hands do not burn. As it cools, keep it moving so it will not stick. After it is cool, cut in small pieces. Serve with a few colored confetti (tiny decorating candies).

3.3.2. Biscotti Amaretti.

The almonds can be sweet or bitter. Usually the majority of farmers plant sweet almonds for many uses. This particular plant is the same shape and color, but has a sour or bitter taste. It can be used for particular cookies, the *amaretti* (sours). This is one of the recipes that many use for Sicilian *biscotti* (biscuits, cookies).

Since the primitive and very ancient times, almonds were used for *biscotti*. In fact, at the time we had more nuns than married women, the monastery was full of young, healthy, beautiful girls. Due to an occupational trade or some love delusion, it was not possible for some young girls to marry the boy her family wanted for her husband. Se would then disobey her family—instead of marrying a man she did not love, she would think it better to become a nun. Another excuse for becoming a nun was that the family had difficulty in giving the *dota* (dowry, money for the wedding) to numerous daughters. Since they were young, the family encouraged the young girl to become a nun, looking for a change to a peaceful life for all the family.

The convent was full of food and it is lucky for the family. Once a week, when going to visit the younger sister in the convent, they would go home with a basket full of *ogni ben di Dio* (all the goods). Some of the nuns were normal and you could see and have contact with them.

Some were *di clausura* (cloistered—not to be seen). They promised fidelity to God. When they got to the convent they had to shave their hair off and were not to have outside contact. They really sacrificed their lives to be nuns. They spent their time doing chores or baking, like making bread and different kings of special *biscotti*. The nuns invented the sour *biscotti*. They would just throw away the sour almonds until they found a way to make a cookie out of the almonds that would have been wasted. They would sell these *biscotti* to the town people to support the convent. They did the sale with a round wooden table with a little window that they called *la sacra ruota* (the sacred wheel). The people would put their money in the wheel and the nun inside would take the money or gift and put the *biscotti* in and turn the table around—all this to prevent them from being seen. Because the people never saw their faces, they would call them by their specialty. They would never give out the recipes because they were very secretive about how the sour almond *biscotti* were made. The sweetest specialty from the convent was called Nun Maria or Nun Rosalie cookie.

But sometimes instead of money or a gift they would find a baby. Maybe the baby was born "unlucky" and a family would not want a scandal, so they preferred to bring the infant to the convent for adoption. Rather than grow up as an orphan, the baby would grow up to be a nun or priest. And maybe after what happened the young girl would listen to the advice of her mother and become a nun to be with her baby.

Life in Sicily was like the sweet and sour almond cookies—it was pure and everything was made from scratch. To become sweet we had to work hard for what we wanted, but the outcome would be good. Like the recipe of the nuns, they would make the most complicated recipe become the most delicious biscotti.

Amaretti Biscotti
Sweet and Sour Biscuits

Ingredients

3 cups flour	1 ½ cup sweet almonds
1 ½ cup roasted bitter almonds	4 eggs, beaten
3 cups sugar	1 teaspoon vanilla
1 lemon peel, grated	1 spoon oil for mixture

Cut the almonds in quarters. Leave a few bitter almonds whole for decoration.

In a large bowl, combine all of the ingredients together. With the spoon of oil, knead the mixture until it becomes a hard dough. Let it rest a little.

Preheat the oven to 375 degrees.

Lightly grease cookie sheets. Shape the mixture one spoonful at a time, in round thick form. Leave a space. Push a bitter whole almond into the center top, about halfway in.

Bake about 25–30 minutes until a light, golden brown and hard.

Transfer to racks and cool completely.

3.3.3. *Biscotti San Martino* (Saint Martin Biscuits).

When the weather starts to be cold and wet, the body requires something hot to feel better. The hot spezie (spices) in Sicily are used whole to give the food a strong taste.

My grandfather ate this biscotti dipped in a glass of red robust wine. He never needed any kind of heat; his body was warm enough.

Ingredients

1 pound heavy semolina (cornmeal)

½ cup hot black peppercorns (whole)

1 cup extra virgin olive oil

1 spoon yeast

1 spoon salt

Pile the semolina on a marble surface. Make a hole in the middle, add the salt and the oil and mix with your hands until it absorbs all the oil. Add the spice. Gradually add the warm water until the mixture becomes hard. Knead the dough for at least 10 minutes to become smooth and elastic.

Flour a surface, cover the dough and leave it to rise for 2 hours. Take pieces of dough and make round biscotto, like doughnuts. Cover and let the dough rise for one hour.

In a large pot, boil 2 quarts water. Put in the biscotto 2 at a time and let them boil for 2 minutes. Lift them out and drain well. Place on a greased oven pan.

Bake in a preheated 400 degree oven to 60 minutes. Turn off the oven and let the biscotti remain in the oven for 30 minutes more until hard, like rust color.

3.3.4. *Cassata siciliana* (Sicilian *ricotta* cake).

This is a rich cake for a complete and festive holiday dinner. In Sicily they make sure to have it on the Easter table. The mother is tired, but proud at the end of the dinner to cut the cake and give a big piece to everyone. The espresso coffee is ready in the small fine porcelain cup with a piece of lemon peel (for the digestion) or for those who like liqueur, a drop of Sambuca.

Filling ingredients:

3 pounds ricotta cheese

1 ½ pounds sugar

2 spoons vanilla

10 pieces diced chocolate

½ cup candied citrus fruits

Sieve the ricotta, drain the excess liquid. Knead with a spatula; blend with the sugar, a little at a time. Add the vanilla and the chocolate. Set aside to rest.

Sponge cake ingredients (prepare the cake the day before)

2 cups cake flour

1 ½ cups sugar

8 eggs (room temperature—take out of refrigerator about 15 minutes before use)

4 spoons baking powder

1 teaspoon lemon juice

1 teaspoon vanilla

4 spoons liqueur (anisette or sambuca)

Preheat the oven to 350 degrees

Separate the eggs. Beat the egg whites until they become thick. Beat the yolk until it is creamy. Mix together.

Add the sugar a little at a time and mix. Add the flour a little at a time and fold in. Add the lemon and vanilla. Mix the baking powder with a spoon of milk and a pinch of sugar. Blend all the ingredients together well.

Place the mixture into a lightly buttered large round cake pan and bake for 45 minutes.

Test with toothpick in center until the toothpick comes out clean and the cake is dry. Remove from oven and cool.

Place in a round heavy dish. Let it rest for a few hours. With a sharp knife, cut the cake horizontally in three layers. Sprinkle each layer with a little anisette or sambuca liqueur. Place 1/3 of the filling onto the first layer, spread with spatula and sprinkle with cocoa powder. Place the second layer on top and repeat. Place the third layer on top and repeat. Garnish with candied citrus fruit. Let cool for a few hours in refrigerator.

You see, in Sicily, even if you buy a small amount of something (because they have so much free time to spend more time to argue than to buy) the customers always complained. The first price asked was always double. When the customer complained, the vendor would begin to justify his high expenses. Finally both were happy and the customer returned home eating the hot roasted chestnuts—making you mouth and body feel warm. That simple food, lingers on my palate still today.

Another winter food for sale on the streets were boiled *carciofini* (small artichokes). The smallest—were only a couple of inches.

They were boiled with salt water, drained and then put into the usual paper cones (plastic did not exist at the time). Before we would arrive home, we would scrape each petal with our teeth throwing the remnants in the street. (At that time we were not thinking about clean streets). We thought that was the "garbage man's" job to clean the next day. We enjoyed eating, walking, talking—not realizing that it was wrong.

Today is another life style. The men that sold these are either too old or have died.

Now the "pizzeria" substitutes for vendor carts. The young people prefer something else. The modern world takes its place with expensive restaurant food, coffee shops. Young people today do not know what fun they missed—or maybe we missed the fun they are having.

I think every generation has its own way of having fun or things to enjoy. But it is hard for the older generations to understand.

3.3.5. Cannoli.

We could only make *cannoli* in the wintertime because the ricotta for filling the *cannoli* shell was only made in the winter season. Maybe it was because the lack of refrigeration made it dangerous to have ricotta sweets. Today thanks to refrigeration we can have this delicious *cannoli* all year long, and enjoy it.

Ingredients for the dough

½ pound white cake flour

½ teaspoon crisco

1 teaspoon dark coffee powder—espresso

1 egg white

1 ¼ teaspoon sugar

1 ½ cup red wine

Ingredients for the filling:

1 pound ricotta cheese, sieved and drained of excess liquid

½ pound powdered sugar

½ pound chopped chocolate (what kind of chocolate?)

½ pound strips of candied orange peel

On a marble surface pile the flour, make a hole in the middle. Add the sugar and coffee powder. Put the Crisco in the hand and allow to melt. Add the wine gradually and mix and knead until it becomes a hard, solid dough. Cover with a kitchen towel and let rest.
Roll with a wood roller until very thin. Cut circles with a plastic coffee can lid. (Use the top of a 1 lb or 13 oz coffee can.)

Wrap the circles around bamboo cane pieces and use foamy egg white to seal the joints. Preheat oil in a deep fry pan and fry the cannoli until browned. Remove from oil and let cool. Remove the cane. (You may also use *cannoli* forms—a metal tube.)

Filling: Knead the ricotta with sugar and chocolate pieces. Blend. With a spoon, fill both ends of the shell and decorate each end with an orange strip.

3.3.6. Zabaglione.

In my youth, I never saw or heard talk about vitamins. Our daily supplement came from the Zabaglione. The wife would get up early and start to beat the fresh (yalk) eggs. She would buy them from a trusted person the day before because they had to be very fresh. She had to keep her husband strong. He had two eggs every morning. The woman would have two eggs. The children had one. We never heard about the problems with cholesterol. We lived in a different world. The yolk of the egg was good, the white thrown out. That reddish smelling cream was camouflaged by a few spoons of sugar and marsala. Nevertheless, it still was unpleasant. If you couldn't swallow it, you could pinch your nose with your fingers and let it go down like a medicine.

Today this is a delicious cocktail, served cold with more ingredients for a better aroma and agreeable taste.

Ingredients

4 egg yolks

1 spoon sugar

½ cup black coffee

½ cup marsala (sweet red wine)

1 lemon peel

1 pinch vanilla

Beat the eggs with the sugar. Add the coffee, marsala, vanilla, and the lemon peel.

Put in a small pot and cook for a few minutes over warm heat, stir until the mixture is creamy.

Put in a serving glass and cover with cocoa powder, cover and let cool for one hour and serve. It is good and you can enjoy it like a soft dessert.

3.3.7. *Pignulata* (Honey balls).

We call this *pignulata*—the ball form of *pigoli*. This is prepared most of the time for Christmas evening.

Dough ingredients

2 cups white flour

4 eggs, beaten (room temperature)

½ cup sugar

1 spoon *anisette*

Ingredients for honey coating

1 cup honey

½ cup sugar

1 spoon cinnamon

On marble surface pile the flour and the sugar. Pour in the eggs. Knead the mixture until it becomes solid and hard. Cover, let rest about ½ hour. Knead the dough again. With your hand, roll and shape the dough into finger-like sticks. Cut ½ inches long and let rest.

Heat oil in a deep electric fry pan. Fry a few at a time for a few minutes until gold. Repeat until all *pignulata* are fried. Remove. Let the oil drain.

In a deep pan, melt the honey with the sugar and cinnamon at a low flame. Place the pieces of *pignulata* into the honey mixture, turning all the time, until they are honey sugar coated (caramelized). Remove. Grease a marble surface and place the honey *pigoli* on it. Wet your hands with fresh water and form the *pigoli* into balls. Place in a colored paper cupcake cup. Allow to cool, and enjoy.

3.3.8. Frutti Matturana (Marzipan).

Frutti Martorana remains one of the most traditional and popular sweet candies in the form of fruit. It is made with a rich paste made with ground almonds. Sugar and egg white cooked together, rolled, colored and worked like a sculpture until it looks like fruit.

Paste Ingredients

1 ½ cups whole blanched sweet almonds

1 ½ cups confectioner's sugar, sifted.

2 egg whites, beaten

Combine the sugar and almonds in a food processor and pulse until they are finely ground. Add the egg white and process until smooth.

Dust the counter with confectioner's sugar. Place the almond paste on the counter, make a well in the center and add the following a little at a time.

3 cups confectioners' sugar, sifted

2 large egg whites, beaten

Knead the mixture until it becomes a smooth paste. Wrap the paste in plastic and cool in the refrigerator. When cool, form small portions into fruit forms, and paint with food coloring to look like fruit. Allow to cool and harden. The candy stays fresh for a long time.

This is the most popular candy for *i morti*, on November 2nd children's holiday.

3.3.9. *Dolci di Natale* (Christmas Cookie).

On the Christmas table, these cookies are so pleasant to look at and so delicious to eat.

Ingredients for the dough

2 pounds cookie flour (Wanda)

½ pound Crisco

1 cup sugar

3 eggs, beaten

1 cup warm milk

1 spoon vanilla

1 spoon baking powder

Ingredients for filling

3 pounds fig marmalade

2 spoons raisins

1 spoon candied fruit, chopped

½ cup honey

1 cup roasted walnuts, finely chopped

½ cup roasted almonds

Grated peel of 2 oranges

Grated peel of 1 lemon

Decorations

1 cup powdered sugar

1 cup colored *confettini* (sprinkles)

On marble surface pile the flour, add the Crisco. Mix with the hands until all the Crisco is absorbed and the flour is greasy. Add a little milk and a pinch of sugar. Gradually add the sugar, the eggs, and the vanilla. Add the milk a little at a time as you knead the dough. Work the dough and knead until all the ingredients are absorbed and the mixture is smooth. Wrap it in a floured towel and let it rest for about 2 hours.

You will need a new single edge razor blade, a small manicure scissors and a plastic cover from a 1 lb/or 13 oz coffee can.

Remove the towel and roll out the dough one piece at a time with a wood rolling pin until the dough is about 1/4 inch thick. With the plastic coffee can cover cut the dough round, fill with a spoon of marmalade, and roll. Place the cookies seam side down on a greased cookie sheet about an inch apart. With the razor blade make a center cut. With the scissors make a few corner cuts like a pinch. Fill the center cut with the colored *confettini*.

Bake for 20–25 minutes in an oven preheated to 375 degrees. Remove to a large dish and sprinkle each cookie with powdered sugar. They are so beautiful and so pleasant to eat.

3.3.10. *Pasticciotti* (Marmalade filled pastry).

This very ancient Sicilian word, "Pasticciotti" means something round, full, and sweet.

These pastries are really like the name.

Every Sicilian city has their own way of doing the different fillings. My town preferred to fill the pastry with their own special *cucuzzata* (Zucchini marmalade)/in summer time the gardener would have their own orto (vegetable garden) with the zucchini plants. After a few weeks they would see that the healthy, long zucchini was ready, they would take the most long and tender ones, and cut it up to become a special marmalade to fill this *pasticciotti*.

Ingredients for marmalade

2 pounds *zucchini*   1 cups ½ sugar

Cut the zucchini; remove all of the hard skin and the seeds. Cut the zucchini in small pieces. Mix with the sugar. Place it in a deep pot. Over a low flame, with a long wood spatula, mix and stir around and around, patiently, for a long time. Turn in the same direction all the time until the sugar is melted and the zucchini pieces start to melt, and little by little become marmalade pieces (not too fine). Cover and let cool a long time.

Ingredients for the dough

2 pounds pastry flour	2 spoons margarine
1 cup sugar	½ pound Crisco
3 beaten eggs	1 spoon baking powder
1 cup milk	1 spoon vanilla

Mix the baking powder with a spoon of milk and a pinch of sugar. On a marble surface, pile the flour. Make a hole in the middle, add the

Crisco, the sugar, the eggs and start to gradually add the milk. Mix with your hands until the flour absorbs the Crisco. Add the vanilla. Knead the mixture well with both hands until it is soft and smooth. Cover with a floured towel and let it rest for at least an hour.

Remove the towel and cut off a piece of the dough. Roll with a wood roller until it is ½ inch thick. With a round plastic coffee cup cut in round pieces. Add one spoon of marmalade on one side of the dough and fold the other side over the dough, half moon shape. Seal. Place in a greased baking pan, leaving one inch between pastries. Continue until the dough is used.

Place in a preheated 375 degree oven and bake for 20 minutes. Remove and cover well with powdered sugar. This pastry will stay fresh in a container for a long time.

After they enjoy it, some person may wonder what kind of marmalade it really is, with this different taste, and ask, "What kind of marmalade is this?" You can answer with pride: It is the pastry confectioner's secret!!!!

3.3.11. *Cuccìa* (Cooked Wheat).

December 13 is Saint Lucia's Day. Like all other Catholic Saints, this is special because she is the eye protector. Traditionally (and the Sicilians have many traditions) that day the Sicilians do not eat bread, but eat the *cuccìa* all day.

Based on wheat, this meal is like minestrone of grain and chick peas, seasoned with honey or, in ancient times, with *vino cotto* (cooked wine).

Ingredients

1 pound wheat grain

½ pound chick peas

½ honey (for seasoning)

Soak the grain in of water the day before. Soak the chick peas for a few hours. Drain. In a big pot with lots of water cook the grain and the chick peas on a low flame for 2 hours or until tender. Add more water if necessary.

Take a few cups, drain, put in a dish and serve with a couple of spoons of honey.

If you want to eat it for dessert, instead of the honey, add 1 cup of ricotta cheese, 2 spoons of sugar and one spoon of chocolate powder and mix. Let it cool in the refrigerator. It is delicious. This is eaten for just one day, for Saint Lucia.

3.3.12. *Torta della domenica* (Sunday Cake).

This was the ancient version of the modern *Tiramisù*. In my young years, I never knew that the mascarpone cream existed. We made the custard cream at home. Because it was easy and economical we had it almost every Sunday to complete the festive family dinner.

Ingredients for the cream

1 quart milk

½ cup sugar

1 lemon rind

6 spoons corn starch (for cooking).

Ingredients for the seasoning

3 cups black coffee, sweet

4 spoons colored *confettini* (sprinkles)

½ cup cocoa (sweet)

1 box lady finger biscotti (cookies)

Prepare the biscotti: Arrange in the bottom of a large deep cake dish. Sprinkle gradually with just enough coffee to make the biscotti soft (not too much— maybe 2 cups).

In a pot, mix the milk and corn starch. Let it dissolve well. Sieve. Make sure it does not have any lumps. Place in another cooking pot.

Add the lemon rind and cook over a low heat, stirring constantly with a wood spoon, making sure the mixture does not burn on the bottom of the pot. Cook until the mixture becomes a soft cream. Remove the lemon rind. Pour the cream on top of the biscotti and sprinkle the cocoa and the *confettini* over the top. Let cool for a few hours in the refrigerator. Serve. Your children are going to be happy.

3.3.13. *Granita di limone* (Lemon Ice).

The first *granita* was served in Sicily many, many years ago. Indeed, this island is so hot and lots of times is invaded by a hot Scirocco wind, it takes one's breath away. The Sicilians had the will power to invent something to refresh the mouth and the body. Nothing can be better than this.

Ingredients

2 ½ quarts water

¾ pounds sugar

The juice of 5 lemons

Boil the water and sugar until sugar is dissolved. Let cool. Add the lemon juice. Pour into plastic ice cube trays and place in the freezer for 2 hours. Remove before it becomes hard ice. Blend in the blender for a few minutes. Place it in a bowl in the freezer again, and stir with a spoon every 20–25 minutes. Return to the freezer until it becomes a sweet, fresh *granita*.

Serve in a glass cup with lemon rind slices and two hard anisette biscotti.

3.3.14. *Granita di caffè con panna* (Whipping cream coffee ice).

This recipe has a refreshing, stronger taste, due to the espresso coffee. This is one of the most sophisticated tastes in a Granita. It will please your palate.

Ingredients

2 cups black coffee (sweet)

½ cup sugar

Juice of four lemons—1 quart water

1 container spray whipping cream (mix in when served)

Make the black coffee, dissolve the sugar. Let cool, add the lemon juice & water.

Place in ice cube trays in freezer. Follow the same directions as the lemon *granita*.

Serve in a long stem crystal glass. Spray the top with whipping cream. Mix the cream with the *granita* and eat immediately. Che delizia!!!

3.3.15. *Granita Mimosa* (Mimosa Ice).

On a hot Sunday morning, when you don't feel like having breakfast and want something different, this is perfect: simple and fresh.

Ingredients
The juice of 5 oranges
½ cup sugar
½ cup water
1 cup champagne

Boil the water, dissolve the sugar. Let cool. Add the orange juice and champagne. Place in an ice cube tray in freezer. Follow the directions for the lemon *granita*.
Serve very soft with a straw. Sip, relax, sit on the terrace and look at the flowers.

3.3.16. *Liquore Limoncello* (Limoncello Liquor).

We used to make our own liquor at home. All of the liquor stores sold the plain alcohol and each family made their own cordial with a different taste. The most famous, delicious, easy and least expensive for us was the *limoncello*. Having a lemon tree in Sicily was like a necessity. Each family had their own lemon tree on the balcony or on a nearby farm. We used lemons in almost every food, for juice, for salad, for cookies, or for this cordial, which, with its special taste, invaded the entire world.

My grandmother had a supply all the time. She kept the little bottle in a cold place on the steps, her special corner. It was ready to serve on a special occasion.

After so many years the young people have discovered the *Limoncello*. I'm so happy!

Ingredients

1 liter 95 proof alcohol (2 ½ quarts)

1 liter water

1 kilo sugar (2 ½ pounds)

12 lemon rinds (cut when the lemon is still green—tender, not ripe) cut very thin. Cut off the white part. Soak the rinds in the alcohol for 10–12 days.)

Boil the water and dissolve the sugar. Take the lemon rinds out of the alcohol and put them in the sugar water. Let cool. Place in preserve jars—the ones with the rubber ring.

In a few weeks, this is a tasty, strong cordial. It can be served as an aperitif with a small amount of ice. For cordial, chill in the refrigerator. The taste is more like the aroma of natural lemon.

3.4. PASTA AND BREAD.

Pasta

For us, the pasta is extremely important, almost sacred, like the bread. *Pasta* can be short, such as *rigatoni, penne, ditalini, farfalle, conchiglie, fusilli*; or very small like *orzo* or *pastina*. The most used ones are long, such as *maccheroncini, spaghetti, spaghettini* and very thin angel hair.

Every day in the early morning my mother started to think what kind of *pasta* she would cook for supper. Every single day the first dish for our 1:00 o'clock dinner was the pasta. All that was changed was the condiment, but it was a dish pasta. Lots of time, especially in the summer, my mother made a fresh *tagliolini* with a little semolina flour (it is important that the flour comes from hard, dark grain), a couple of glasses of warm water, a pinch of salt. It would be kneaded together to make a hard dough, and worked hard until the dough became elastic.

Then she would take a piece, and start to stretch it with the wood roller until it became a large round size. She rolled all the dough around the roller and cut the middle length-wise. With a sharp knife she would cut it to ½ inches wide and hang on a long bamboo cane to dry for a couple of hours. She did this in the early morning and it was ready to cook for the 1:00 dinner time. It would be seasoned with a fresh tomato salsa, and the top would be garnished with two slices of fried eggplant, basil leaves and a spoonful of fresh grated cheese. We did not need an entrée; this is a complete dinner.

She made fresh *maccheroncini* too, with the same dough, but in a different shape. She used la "Busa", a thin strand of grain, to make the hole in the thin macaroni.

In the wintertime it was the appropriate *minestra* (soup). We used the vegetables or beans we had at home. We always had lentils and *fave* in the house to prepare some hot soup, or cool *minestra* depending on the temperature of the day. The appropriate pasta was short like *ditalini* of crushed *capellini* (Yes, we could also use a long pasta, cut first with the hands, put inside a kitchen towel, covered and crushed.)

Bread. The first time I made bread was with my grandmother when I was a child. We were in the countryside, and we made it in the *forno a legna* (wood oven). It was a hot burning stove heated with dried wood branches of the old trees. At the right time, when the burning stove had the right temperature, the ashes of the wood fire would be cleaned out of the oven and the bread would be placed in the oven, one by one, with a wood stick with a very long handle. The bread would be cooked for at least half an hour, and the nice, hot bread with the most desirable aroma would be taken out.

Our people spent a lot of time cooking and eating fresh products. Bread, cheese and wine would be put on big ceramic plates that had many cracks from many generations use. The meals would be seasoned with wild herbs and extra virgin olive oil made with our olives, and put in jars. It was always ready to be used.

When we got up in the morning, our first thought was what we were going to make for lunch and dinner, and we organized our day in such a way that allowed us to go to the fresh market and buy fresh products for our meals. I am hoping to hand down these traditions to my grandchildren. I have already invited them home to make fresh bread together. I already taught them how to measure the ingredients and make the dough. They showed a lot of interest and overall they had a lot of fun with me!!!

3.4.1. Homemade bread.

I want to start my recipes with the bread. Like the Pater Noster (Our Father) prayer says, "Give us the daily bread." For us, this is the most important daily food.

In my youth, my mother made enough bread once a week for the whole family. She kneaded all that flour (a lot), was patient, and loved to make all the round bread, put it up to rise, and wait until it was ready. She prepared the wood for the brick oven to bake. The early morning for us was hard work, and in the meantime we would eat pizza, Brusketta (hot bread), and fresh bread. During the holiday season when the oven was still hot we did the cookies. That hard work became a celebration.

Ingredients

5 cups all-purpose flour

2 pkg active dry yeast

1 ½ cups warm water

2 tablespoons oil

2 teaspoons salt

Empty the yeast into a bowl with a little almost cold water. Stir and dissolve the yeast. Add salt, one spoon oil. A little at a time, add the flour and water, gradually. Mix with hands (It is easy and better.) until well blended.

Transfer the dough to a lightly floured surface, and knead from all corners until smooth and elastic. Rub the top with a little oil, cover, let rise in warm place for about 2 hours, until double.

Cut the dough in a few pieces, flour the surface and knead and roll into a round form. Place in oiled and floured baking pans situated in a warm place (under a kitchen towel). Cover and let rise again, 30 minutes or more, until mature.

Preheat the oven for 20 minutes, to 425. Bake for 40 minutes. When done, bottom crust will look gold. Remove from pan and cool.

If you desire a *bruschetta,* make cuts in the middle of the bread, sprinkle with virgin olive oil, salt and pepper and grated cheese. Return to the oven for a few minutes. Delicious.

3.4.2. *Pizza.*

Pizza is one of the best known foods in the world. When people taste it, they love and eat it. It comes in many varieties, good for breakfast, lunch and dinner.

Crust

6 cups flour	3 envelopes yeast
2 cups warm water	2 spoons oil
½ spoon sugar	½ spoon salt.

Soften the yeast and the sugar in a half glass of water. Combine 3 cups flour, water, yeast mixture and salt. Mix in a large bowl until blended. With a wood spoon, stir in 2 more cups flour. On a floured surface, knead the dough for 10 to12 minutes, adding the rest of the flour until the dough is soft and smooth and does not stick to the surface. Divide the dough in half and shape into balls. Cover and let rise in a warm place for 60 to 90 minutes, until double.

Grease 2 large pizza sheets with ½ spoon oil and a little flour. Stretch one ball of dough on each. Cover and let rise until double again.

Condiment

16 of fresh cherry tomatoes (or peeled.)

1 finely chopped onion

½ cup grated Romano cheese

2 spoons minced garlic

8 salt sardines (in oil)

½ spoon salt

¼ spoon oregano

¼ spoon pepper

6 leaves basil

Oven temperature: 375 degrees

Crush tomatoes (not juice) salt, pepper. Spread the sauce on the pizza crust. Sprinkle the garlic, grated cheese, oregano, basil leaves and

sardines in pieces. Finish with a lot of extra virgin olive oil. Bake in a
hot oven for 25 minutes. Serve immediately, with a glass of wine!!!!!

3.4.3. *Minestra di cucuzza* (Squash soup).

For minestra (soup), our people are taught that each family has their
own version and specialty. The ministra for us then was a substitute for
heat, especially in the cold days we looked for some hot meal to heat the
room and the body. It was economical too. For a little money the whole
family gets full. There are so many kinds of zucchini. We use the long
yellow "baseball bat" zucchini. For us it is the best.

Ingredients

1 zucchini—2 pounds

2 potatoes, finely cut

4 fresh scallions, chopped

4 leaves basil

4 minced garlic cloves

2 peeled tomatoes

2 fresh sage leaves

2 spoons fresh grated parmesan cheese

2 stock cubes, salt and pepper

Peel off the hard squash skin with a sharp knife. Cut through the
middle, lengthwise and take out all the seeds. Wash and cut in small 1
inch pieces.

In a deep pot, sauté the onion and potatoes in abundant oil. Add the
zucchini and stir. Cook for about 5 minutes. Add in the crushed tomatoes and herbs. Let the tomatoes start to melt to pink sauce. Dissolve
the stock cubes in a glass of water and add to the mixture. Let it absorb
for a few minutes. Add water until it is about 1 inch over the zucchini

and simmer. Add salt and pepper. If you like, add a pinch of powdered red pepper. Let cook on a low flame until the zucchini is tender.

Cook ½ pounds angel hair pasta, crushed. Drain, leave a little juice. Combine the zucchini mixture and pasta and let the flavors combine together.

Sprinkle a spoon of fresh parmesan on top of the dish.

3.4.4. *Timballo di Bucatini* (Bucatini Cake).

The first baked pasta I ate was in the late 50's. I saw the first gas oven in the kitchen of my fiancé's home. My mother in law really loved to cook. She was a kitchen fanatic. She used so many modern kitchen utensils. She was so good at preparing different dishes with many ingredients, and prepared many sophisticated dinners.

As soon as we were engaged, she invited me almost every Sunday. Most of the time she prepared a fish dinner. All of the family loved fish the most, and she did it in so many different ways. For the special holiday, she invited my parents too, and she proudly prepared her specialties. One of them was the *timballo* which was baked in the gas oven. This was a little round over a little bigger than a regular cake pan, similar to a small round micro oven. We put the pan full of pasta or cake, or something else inside the little dish in the oven, situated in the top of the regular gas range. The medium low flame was lit and the oven slowly would go around and cook (or dry) the pasta. Once in a while we checked to see if it was ready. The oven didn't show the time or temperature—we decided the time by sight.

It was such a luxury to possess the gas oven after so many years of cooking with the olive branch fire. Finally we could keep the kitchen clean and not have so much mess, or so much work!!! This was fast and clean. Everything in America is fast, modern. We just call it American style.

Ingredients

1 pound *bucatini*	½ pound chopped meat
½ pound fresh peas	4 ounces *mortadella*
3 hard boiled eggs	1 beaten egg
½ cup fresh grated *pecorino Romano* cheese	
3 minced garlic cloves	1 28 ounce can peeled tomatoes
4 fresh basil leaves	Salt and pepper

In a deep pot, prepare the salsa. Sauté the garlic until gold. Add in the peas and sauté, Blend the tomatoes in. Add salt, pepper and basil and start to cook at high flame. When it boils, lower the heat.

In a frying pan, sauté the chopped meat. Drain. Add to the deep pot. Let cook until the sauce is thick.

Cut the boiled eggs in quarters. Cut the *mortadella* in small pieces.

Boil the *bucatini* 7 minutes (al dente). Drain well. Add the salsa with the peas. (not too liquid)

Put the pasta in a baking pan. Add the eggs and *mortadella*. On the top sprinkle the beaten egg, sprinkle the cheese.

Preheat the oven to 350 and cook for 15 minutes until it sticks together like a *timballo*. Serve cut in pieces, like a cake. This pasta is convenient for a picnic, easy to carry and serve.

3.4.5. *Pasta con le sarde.*

This is the most important pasta dish for the *Saccensi*, the inhabitants of Sciacca. Every town, and every family has its own way to make it, and no one gives their recipe to anyone else. Some make just green salsa, my mother made it with lots of red (in the tomatoes) and green (in the fennel) salsa.

Ingredients

2 pounds fresh boned sardines

2 pounds fresh wild fennel

2 spoons raisins, soaked for a few minutes in water.

2 spoons pine nuts, cut in half

1 spoon minced parsley

2 cups bread crumbs

2 finely sliced white onions

2 minced garlic cloves

4 sardine fillets (dry salted)

1 18-ounce can crushed tomatoes

3 strands fresh saffron (or a pinch of dried saffron)

2 bay leaves

1 pound macaroni *fusilli*, or *perciatelli*

Boil the fennel in salt water for 8 minutes, drain, cut in pieces. Keep the green water for boiling the pasta later.

In virgin olive oil, sauté the garlic and the onions, add the dry sardines, the tomatoes, salt and pepper, and let it boil for 10 minutes. Add the fennel, the fresh sardines, and all of the other ingredients. Let boil, lower the heat, and cook for another 25 minutes.

Toast the bread crumbs, turning frequently, to a golden color in a frying pan (no oil).

Boil the pasta for 6 minutes (al dente). It should still be firm. Drain well. Remove the bay leaves from the salsa. Put the pasta in an oven pan, top with the salsa and then the toasted bread crumbs, reserving a few spoonsful of crumbs for the end.

Heat the oven to 350 degrees. Bake the dish for 15 minutes and serve hot. Put the reserved bread crumbs on top of the pasta instead of grated cheese.

If you have not eaten this before, I am sure you will want to eat it soon again.

3.4.6. *Pasta fritta* (fried *pasta*).

The only people in my town in Sicily who owned a refrigerator before 1961 were the fancy restaurants or salumeria (delicatessen). In the movies I saw a rich family had the refrigerator, not in the kitchen, but in the dining room like a piece of fancy furniture.

It was small, white, with a single door and a metal handle. Inside there were a couple of compartments. On the top shelf there was a small compartment for the basket where the ice was made. No one thought of frozen food yet. On the bottom shelf there were a few bottles of water or *aranciata* (orangeade).

Like I said before, we never possessed a refrigerator at home. I did not know that no one had one. Some people had a TV, but no refrigerator. Those were the years when everything was measured, controlled: spending money, shopping, cooking, eating, etc.

When my mother cooked, she knew exactly the amount of pasta she wanted for boiling. She measured with her hands. We rarely had anything left over. If we had some we would eat it at night for *cena* (supper), especially if it was pasta with salsa—it was really a treat if we had *pasta fritta* on lots of pure olive oil. For the soup and salad, we used the new oil from the recent harvest. For frying we used the oil that remained from the years before, and we were not happy because we thought it was not the same.

After I came to America the eating style changed. All of the people started to use the vegetable oil, thinking that the olive oil was too strong. After a few years, after a lot of people already had high cholesterol, a few doctors started to approve the modern expression: "The best oil is the extra virgin olive oil." Today they add the word "Extra Virgin." What a beautiful word. Except today it does not exist in this world. Almost nothing is honest and pure. That's the sad part. Unfortunately they seek for something like this beautiful word, "virgin" in just the olive oil and wool material. Otherwise this word does not exist.

I saw I had my first refrigerator when I came to America. It was old, small and white, exactly like the one I had seen so many years before in the film. Still, in the beginning, I did not believe in frozen food. We used it just for cold water and to save some food. I was still not americanized yet and I tried to go shopping for food every night when I returned from work and cooked fresh meal. For two people, it was fast and easy.

Even my mother in Sicily, after a few years she had to start to be modern in the dining room to be comfortable any place. Not like America. In America everything they got is big and disproportionate. (Even worse than night and day.) In the other side of the world, places still exist where they have everything older and smaller and they are still happy.

3.4.7. *Pasta Carrittera* o al pesto (Pesto pasta, oil and garlic).

We call pasta "Carrettera" after the people who work driving horse carriages. After a long day working at driving the horse and carriage, especially in the summertime under the sun, they arrive home late in the night, tired. They don't have the time and patience to wait a long time to have a fancy supper prepared. They prefer an easy dish pasta like this one. It is ready in a few minutes, tastes nice, and is healthy.

We still prefer this dish pasta sometimes late at night with a group of friends. Instead of making another cup of coffee, this Carrettera is a healthy and easy to make dish pasta. The men at the table talk or play cards and the women prepare the dish and continue to talk in the kitchen. We stay together longer, have an extra glass of wine, especially on the weekend.

Ingredients

1 pound spaghettini

8 cloves garlic

4 mature cherry tomatoes (cut)

4 spoons fresh grated parmesan cheese

8 leaves fresh basil

½ glass extra virgin olive oil

Salt and pepper

In a mortar pound the garlic with ½ teaspoon salt, the basil, the tomatoes, the olive oil, a pinch (or more if you like it hot) of hot red pepper.

Boil the spaghettini, drain and leave a little pasta broth.

Pour into a dip pasta bowl, add the butter, pesto the cheese, serve it very hot and enjoy!!!

3.4.8. Potato and pea pasta.

This dish is so easy and fast to prepare and so good to eat. You can make your own version. If you want just vegetables, don't use *prosciutto*; use peas and potatoes.

Ingredients

1 pound pasta *farfalle*

½ pound small frozen peas

¼ pound chopped *prosciutto*

1 large diced potato

1 chopped sweet white onion

2 leaves fresh sage

1 cup stock

3 spoons caci

2 spoons buttero cavallo cheese

Salt and pepper

Put four spoons extra virgin olive oil and 2 spoons butter in a frying pan. Sauté the onion, potatoes and at the end, the *prosciutto*. Add the peas and a little salt (the *prosciutto* is salty).

Add the stock, a little at a time. add the sage leaves. Cook on a low flame until the potatoes are tender. Remove the sage leaves.

Boil the *farfalle*. Drain. Combine the pasta and the sauce in a pasta bowl and let them absorb each other for a few minutes.

Add the cheese, mix and serve immediately.

FISH

Because Sciacca is a city next to the sea, the markets are full of fish all of the time. Since early in the morning, the young fish men return to the port with the basket full of fish. The young fish men are ready. You can buy a few baskets at a good price. They display a few fish in a dish. They don't need a scale. They start to sell the fish shouting in a loud voice through the streets that they have the best fish at the best price. They are really fresh, but maybe not the best quality or size, but the most fresh.

Most of the good fish from our sea are: Merluzzo (cod), Triglie (red snapper). Sardines (anchovies), Anquille (eel), Sogliole (filet of Sole), polipo (Octopus), Calamari (Squid), Seppie (Sepia), Ganberi (Shrimp), Pesce spada (Swordfish), Tonna (Tuna).

Tuna is caught in the *tonnara*, a special space in the sea. The fishermen first tried to fish with the adequate net, and afterward on top of the water. A fight started between the fishermen and the tuna that tried to get away with its life.

This is a traditional fair in Sicily, and is called *mattanza* (tuna killing). It is upsetting to see the fishermen pulling the net and trying to kill the big fish with a long bat. The fish struggles with its long tail, and tried to escape. The see water became red with blood. More fishermen came to help (the fish are really big). After a heavy fight, finally they pull that big fish into the boat, then try to calm it down for a few more minutes. The fish still moves its tail and little by little, situated in the ice, is ready for the market (I'm sure after seeing that, nobody would want to eat any more tuna). Unfortunately, we try to forget that, because the meat tastes delicious.

3.5.1. *Pesce spada* (Swordfish).

Sicilian Style

At our marina (Mediterranean Sea) the swordfish is often available fresh in a few months of the year or frozen in the others. It is not really cheap, but affordable. We needed just a few pieces mixed with tasty natural herbs and it became a most sophisticated culinary dish to satisfy the whole family

Ingredients

6 slices boned swordfish

4 minced garlic cloves

1 finely sliced white onion

1 stick celery, finely sliced

½ glass white wine

1 spoon capers (washed, or leave salted for a stronger taste)

2 spoons green olives (pitted and chopped)

6 leaves fresh basil

2 bay leaves

4 mint leaves

2 spoons fresh finely chopped basil

½ spoon oregano

6 mature tomatoes (or peeled) chopped

½ cup flour (to coat the fish)

2 spoons butter

Clean and salt the fish, coat with flour on both sides. Heat oil and butter in a fry pan, and lightly fry the fish on both sides. Place fish to the side.

Sauté the onion and the garlic, add the tomatoes. In a few minutes, add the fish, sprinkle with the wine (little by little), and cover with the tomatoes. Add the herbs and the other ingredients, salt and pepper. Cover. Allow to boil for a few minutes. Lower the flame and cook for 15 more minutes and serve with a red *pastoso* (dinner) wine.

The aroma is so good that it will make your mouth impatient, until you finally taste it.

3.5.2. *Insalata di polipo* (Octopus salad).

On the Christmas nightly table it is almost obligatory to have this fish salad, tasty and traditional. The most tender and good are the smallest. You can cook and serve the entire octopus.

Ingredients

2 pounds octopus

6 minced garlic cloves

4 finely chopped fresh scallions

juice of two lemons

½ cup virgin olive oil

4 mint leaves

2 spoons finely chopped parsley

6 leaves fresh basil

1 spoon oregano

Clean the fish with fresh water. Remove the eye in the middle. Leave all the tentacles. In a large pot, boil enough water to cover the fish. Put the tentacles in and lift in and out until the tentacles are curled, then put the entire octopus down in the pot, and boil for 30 minutes. If the octopus is large, it will need more cooking time.

Shut off the flame. Leave the fish inside the covered pot 20 minutes more, to tenderize.

Drain, cut in pieces. Place in a large salad bowl with the other ingredients, and let it absorb the oil and lemon juice. Serve for salad or for *antipasto*.

3.5.3. *Baccalà a la ghiotta* (Dry salted codfish).

This the largest codfish. After the catch they put it in a special salt and very cold temperature to dry for a long time.

The perfect time to do this *ghiotta* (stew) is in the winter time. It is perfect for Christmas. My father loved it, so my mother served it often. The fish was sold entirely dry and it required a long process to become soft. We would cut the fish in pieces and soak it for a few days in a lot of fresh water. The water was changed every day so the fish would become soft and smell better. Finally after a few days it will start to be soft and ready to cook. They are sold already soft, so this is the best way to buy it. This strange but very good fish is worth to be cooked and tasted.

Ingredients

2 pounds *baccalà*

1 cup black olives

½ stick celery, finely sliced

2 spoons fresh finely chopped parsley

¼ cup capers (washed)

1 spoon oregano

1 pound potatoes, cut up

2 onion slices

¼ cup dry red wine

1 can crushed tomatoes

Pepper (less salt because the fish is salted)

½ cup flour to coat the fish

Wash the fish well to make sure the salt is all out. Dry coat with flour on all sides. In a deep pan, fry it in olive oil. In the same oil fry the potatoes and sauté all of the other ingredients. Add the oregano and parsley last. Add the tomatoes and let cook for a few minutes, then add ½ glass water to let the potatoes cook until tender. Arrange the fish pieces one at a time. Sprinkle the wine on top, add salt (very little) and pepper. Cover with tomato salsa and let cook for 10 minutes more. Serve hot. This is tender and delicious.

3.5.4. *Rinaloru in agrodolce* (Little shark, sweet and sour).

This is made with a very small young shark, almost pink in color. After the dark heavy skin is taken off, this becomes a delicious tasting exotic Sicilian dish.

In Sicily, almost everything we cook we fix with agro dolce (sweet and sour). Yes, like the life in Sicily, we try the most sour thing, like vinegar, with a pinch of sugar so it became almost sweet. It is not really sweet, but is a different, better, sweet and sour taste.

Ingredients

2 pounds fish

2 chopped red onions

½ cup green olives, pitted and chopped

¼ cup capers (salted)

4 crushed garlic cloves

1 glass red vinegar

1 spoon sugar

½ glass water

4 leaves fresh basil

½ cup chopped parsley

½ cup flour to coat the fish

1 can tomato paste, diluted with same amount of water

1 spoon oregano

6 leaves fresh mint

4 leaves fresh marjoram

Buy the fish with the skin off and cleaned. Cut in small pieces. Wash well with fresh water. Dry every piece, salt and coat with flour. Fry in deep olive oil. Remove the fish. Remove the frying oil.

In clean oil sauté the onion and garlic. Add a teaspoon of vinegar and the diluted tomato paste and cook a few minutes. Add the vegetables, herbs and fish. Dilute the vinegar with ½ glass water and the sugar. Mix until the sugar melts. Sprinkle little by little on top of the fish, salt, oregano, pinch of red pepper. Cover. Let cook for a few minutes on a high flame, then lower the flame and cook 15 minutes more. Serve with a loaf of Italian bread and a glass of wine. Sip a cup of espresso coffee.

3.5.5. Brodo di pesce (Fish soup).

On a cold winter night, nothing is better than a hot fish soup. You can use almost every fish found in the market. The best in our opinion was the small merluzzi (whiting) or shrimp.

Ingredients

1 pound whiting

1 pound shrimp

1 pound filet of sole

1 pound

6 chopped garlic cloves

8 mature chopped cherry tomatoes

2 spoons chopped parsley

salt and pepper

1 cup rice

Sauté the garlic, add the tomatoes. After a few minutes add 6 cups of water. (My mother never used fish stock.) Let boil 5 minutes. Add all the fish, add the parsley, let boil 20 minutes. Remove the fish and take out the spine and bones.

In a pot, sauté the rice with a little virgin oil. Add the liquid from the fish, a little at a time until the rice is tender (if the rice needs more liquid, use hot water). Cut the fish in small pieces and add it to the rice. Add a pinch of extra salt and pepper. Serve hot with a little broth.

If you use bread, then you have a lovely soup. You could use the broth to cook a tasteful rise or *pastina*.

3.5.6. Sarde *a chiappa* (Coupled sardines).

Sardines in my home town are the most abundant fish on the market. They are small and very tasty, which depends on the quality of the sea.

Ingredients

2 pounds sardines (remove the head, cut the fish lengthwise and remove the backbone with your thumb.

1 cup seasoned bread crumbs

2 teaspoons wild fennel seeds

1 spoon finely chopped parsley

2 spoons finely chopped mint

1 glass extra virgin oil (to deep fry the fish)

1 beaten egg

6 bay leaves

Juice of one lemon

Mix the bread crumbs with the parsley, fennel and garlic. Dip each filet in the olive oil and coat with the seasoned bread crumbs. Put two fish together tightly, dip in the beaten egg and coat again with the bread crumbs. Arrange the paired fish in a greased baking pan and cover with bay leaves. Sprinkle with a little more oil and a drop of lemon. Bake in a 350 degree preheated oven for 15 minutes. This tastes good when cooled a little. Eat together with a few pieces of white sweet onions. The taste is exalted when you fry them—in that case you cover them with flour.

3.5.7. Spigola arrostita (Roasted seabass)

The best fish for barbecue is the seabass, marinated and cooked with charcoal over a high flame. With one simple pesto sauce, it became a distinguished supper with a very Mediterranean taste.

Ingredients

3 seabass

8 minced garlic cloves

Juice of 4 lemons

4 spoons chopped parsley

6 leaves chopped mint

1 spoon *pinoli*, chopped very small

1 spoon almonds, chopped fine

4 spoons chopped basil

1 spoon oregano

1 cup extra virgin olive oil

Pesto: Place the garlic and a spoon of salt in an old mortar, pound down and squeeze until the garlic "melts". Add the parsley, pound down. Add the basil, mint, *pinoli*, almonds and pound fine. Add the oil, lemon juice and oregano. Mix them all.

Heat the barbecue. Clean the fish. With a sharp knife, make two traverse slashes on each side of the fish. Put a spoonful of the pesto inside each cut. Put the fish on a large sheet of aluminum foil and make a few holes in the foil. Cover with foil. Place on the grill.

Close the top of the grill, and let it cook for 20 minutes. Open one side of the foil and let it roast for 5 more minutes. Take the fish from the foil and display on a rectangular dish. Add the rest of the pesto and serve. The pesto will fill your room with a pleasant garlic and lemon aroma. Before cooking is done, when you set the table, don't forget to prepare a bottle of white wine!!!

3.5.8. Calamari ripieni (stuffed squid).

The largest squid is preferred, white and whole. Make sure it does not have any holes in the stomach. They need a little more work and time, but it is worth it. They are very good.

Ingredients

1 cup of Rice

12 squid

6 cloves garlic

½ cup black olives, pitted and chopped

4 hard boiled eggs

2 cups flour (to coat the fish)

¼ cup fresh grated parmesan cheese

2 spoons finely chopped parsley

2 cans 28 ounce peeled tomatoes (blend)

salt and pepper, and pinch of red pepper

Boil the rice in salt water until very tender. Add a spoon of butter and let cool.

Clean the squid inside and outside. Put on a large, flat dish. Cut off the tentacles.

In a frying pan sauté the garlic, the olives and the tentacles. Add to the rice.

Cut the eggs in quarters and mix with the rice. Mix in the parsley, salt and pepper.

Take a spoonful of the rice mixture and lightly stuff each squid from the open side.

(Gives a little room to cook and it will not break open.)

Close the opening with a toothpick and cover each squid with flour. In a frying pan, fry the squid 2 minutes each side. Handle gently so it does not open.

In another pan, prepare the tomato sauce. Let it boil for five minutes. Place the squid one by one in the sauce. Let cook for 20 minutes more and serve each piece with the sauce on top.

MEAT

It was not an important food for us, since fish was important, but meat was and still is a necessary food in the traditionally religious feasts, as well as in *Carnevale* or during a party in the country with friends.

3.6.1. Arancine di riso (rice balls).

The rice balls have this name because the balls are round and orange.

My mother-in-law was a *maestra* (teacher) in making this dish. On every special occasion or holiday, she would prepare it the day before and have it ready for the antipasto. Every time we would visit some relative, if she would not bring it, they would ask for it because they were accustomed to receiving it. She had a special way to prepare and cook it.

Every special new dish she would see, she would try to make it. Even if you asked, no one would give you the right recipe, so she would try to guess the right ingredients, and she did it. She taught me how to make these *arancine*.

In Sicily, when it is time to give a recipe to someone, they become the enemy. No one told the truth. Everyone kept their secret recipes for a family secret. So each one would have to learn to do it in her own way—try and try again, and finally the proud boast: They do it the best!!!

Ingredients (for about 16 rise balls)

1 ½ cup rice

2 eggs (for the mixture)

½ cut fresh grated cheese

2 spoons of butter

8 ounces chopped meat

8 ounces sausage (out of the skin)

8 ounces small peas (green peas?)

salt, pepper

Ingredients for the salsa

1 16 ounce can peeled tomatoes

1 8 ounce can tomato paste

4 finely minced garlic cloves

Ingredients for coating

4 beaten eggs

2 cups bread crumbs

½ cup flour

½ cup cheese (what kind?)

Vegetable oil for deep frying (about ½ gallon)

Boil the rice in 4 quarts water for 15 minutes. Add the butter. Cover and let cool.

Prepare the thick sauce.

In another large pot, sauté the garlic, meat and sausage. Puree the tomatoes and add. Dilute the tomato paste with double the amount of water. Add and let boil. Add the peas. Let cook 25–30 minutes on a low heat, until it thickens.

Remove the meat and the peas from the sauce and keep in a separate dish with a little sauce.

In a large container mix the rice, the eggs, the cheese, and salt and pepper. Take ½ cup of the sauce and put in the rice mixture. Mix until it becomes an orange color.

Prepare the coating mix: Beat the eggs. In another dish, mix the bread crumbs, the flour and the cheese.

Prepare the rice balls: Take a spoonful of the rice mixture and place it in your palm. Take another spoon of meat and peas, and put it on the rice mixture. Take another spoonful of the rice mixture and put it on top. Close firmly and shape into a tight ball.

Dip in the beaten egg and coat with the bread crumbs. Roll well to become a good hard rice ball. Repeat with the rest of the rice and meat.

Heat the oil in a fry pan heated to 350 degrees. Fry the rice balls a few at a time, for 7 to 10 minutes until they become golden brown. Place on a rack to drain the excess oil. Serve.

I hope you enjoy eating this as much as we love to bring this special recipe to you.
Sicilian: Homemade rice balls "Hat-Off".

3.6.2. Crocchette di broccoli e salsiccia (Sausage and *broccoli* croquettes).

These are the most preferred croquettes. I make these almost every holiday, or every time I have company. You want to spend a few hours with friends, sip a glass of wine and chat.

If you prefer, spinach may be used instead of broccoli. They are both good.

Ingredients

1 bunch of broccoli florets	6 eggs, beaten (for the dip)
5 potatoes (boiled and mashed)	2 cups bread crumbs (for coating)

6 pieces sweet sausage (skin removed)   6 pieces hot sausage (skin removed)

2 eggs, beaten (for the mixture)   ½ cup bread crumbs (for the mixture)

2 cups fresh grated cheese   6 minced garlic cloves

2 spoons butter   pinch of salt

pinch of black or red pepper

Boil the broccoli florets for 5 minutes. Drain. Cut in small pieces.
Cut the sausage in small pieces. Sauté.
Add the broccoli and garlic and sauté for a few minutes.

In a large, deep dish, mix the mashed potatoes, 2 eggs, ½ cup bread crumbs and cheese.
Add the sausage, broccoli, garlic, salt and pepper. Mix well.

Take a large spoon of the mixture. Dip into the beaten eggs and coat with bread crumbs.
Roll it with your palms into a oval croquette form.

Fry in deep oil on both sides for a few minutes. Drain the excess oil on paper towels.

3.6.3. Coniglio in agrodolce (Sweet and sour rabbit).

Hunting in Sicily is one of the oldest sports for young and old men alike. As soon as hunting season is open, they go in the early morning with the guns over their shoulder, and start to look for some wild rabbits.

Ingredients

1 rabbit   ¼ cup capers

½ cup green olives   ½ cup red wine

4 minced garlic cloves

6 leaves parsley, finely chopped

1 white onion, finely chopped

¼ cup red wine vinegar

½ spoon oregano

4 potatoes, cut in quarters

4 sprigs rosemary

1 stick celery, chopped

8 red ripe tomatoes, peeled and chopped

1 spoon sugar

4 bay leaves

½ cup flour

1 extra glass vinegar, for marinade (how much?)

One lemon (the whole lemon, or the juice?)

1 glass oil (how much?)

4 mint leaves

Cut the rabbit in pieces and wash well in salt water. Rinse. Rub the meat with the lemon juice. Marinate for 2, 3 hours or more in vinegar, oil, oregano and ½ glass water.

Rinse, drain. Coat the rabbit with flour and fry. Dilute the vinegar with ½ glass water, add the sugar. Sprinkle on top of the meat and allow to evaporate on high heat. Add the other ingredients, the tomatoes, a glass of water, salt and pepper. Cook on a low flame for an hour or more, until tender. Very tasty.

3.6.4. *Salsiccia con olive* (Olive sausage).

This is an old Sicilian recipe we prepared for New Year's Eve. The frying pork filled the room with aroma. We would set the table and the company would arrive. The wine bottles were full. The black olives were harvested the year before by my mother with love and patience. On a hot summer days they would be spread out in a wicker basket in the sun and dried. The extra oil from the olives would drip through the basket. Every day, before they were spread out in the sun they would be sprinkled with a few spoons of marine salt and mixed frequently to let the excess oil drip.

Day by day they would get more dry until they became "Passaluna (black dry). After so many days turning and tending, at the end of the summer they became sweet, dry and ready to eat (in the beginning they are very bitter).

The pork sausage in the winter is very economical and healthy. With a couple of pieces and half dozen olives for each person you can have a nice family meal.

Ingredients

10 pieces sweet pork sausage	2 pieces hot pork sausage
24 (or more) dry black olives	6 minced garlic cloves
1 glass red wine	6 leaves marjoram
3 lemons, quartered	

Wash the salt off the olives.

Put the sausages in a deep pan. Prick them with a fork a few times and pour in the wine. Let the wine evaporate, and turn the sausages several times until the wine is almost gone. Drain the rest of the wine.

In the same pan, add ¼ cup oil and fry the sausages, both sides until they are a golden color. Sprinkle in the herb, add the olives and lightly fry them. Add the garlic at the end and fry until golden, for a few minutes.

Serve each dish with a couple of pieces of cut lemon to squeeze on the sausage after it is cut in half lengthwise. Let the lemon juice be absorbed.

Enjoy this different supper with a loaf of semolina bread…and a glass of dry wine!!!

3.6.5. Capretto al forno (roast lamb).

At least once a year, for Easter, like in the Catholic tradition, cook a young lamb. The best tasting way to roast the lamb is in the hot wood country oven, but today it is not possible to do that anymore. We happily arranged to do it in the gas or electric range. If we have a barbecue stove, it is easy just to roast the leg of lamb with a few aromatic herbs, oil, lemon and garlic.

Capretto (milk lamb) is more tender and can be cooked whole. The meat tastes excellent.

Ingredients

5 pound *capretto* (milk lamb)	1 pound small whole red potatoes
1 pound fresh peas	6 scallions (cut long pieces)
½ glass rosé wine (half for steam)	½ glass rose wine (for cook later)
1 spoon chopped parsley	1 stick chopped celery
½ pound small whole carrots	4 sprigs rosemary
8 whole bay leaves	6 garlic cloves (whole)
12 minced garlic cloves	1 spoon oregano
Juice of two lemons	salt and pepper
½ glass pure oil (for marinade)	4 spoons butter

Use half of the herbs for marinade, half for cooking.

Wash the meat in fresh water. Cut off the excess fat (not all, leave some). Cut the lamb in pieces.

The day before, marinate the meat with the oil, lemon juice, whole cloves garlic, half of the herbs, salt and pepper. Cover and refrigerate.

Preheat the oven to 400 degrees.

Drain the marinade.

In a deep frying pan, sauté the meat pieces on all sides in oil. Add the other half of the herbs and the garlic, and sprinkle with wine, a little at a time. Let the wine evaporate. Remove the meat to a large roasting pan (not the wine). Add the herbs, the potatoes and peas.

Sprinkle with a little olive oil. Put the butter on top of the meat. Add the cleaned wine, 1 glass water. Add salt, pepper and oregano. Cover with aluminum foil and let bake for one hour.

Remove the foil and taste the potatoes. If they are tender, make sure there is enough liquid. If not, put in a little more water, cover again and cook more.

With the meat and vegetable liquid, you can season a dish of *ditalini* pasta.

3.6.6. Pollo in brodo (Chicken soup).

Some times in the winter, on a very cold season holiday, instead of starting the festive dinner with antipasto, we started the dinner with a broth. It was something light to prepare the stomach. The easiest, quickest and good tasting is chicken soup.

Ingredients

1 chicken	2 cups peas
1 stick chopped celery	4 chopped red tomatoes
3 potatoes, quartered	2 cups carrots, cut up
1 white onion, chopped	4 spoons basil
1 sprig rosemary	6 whole black peppercorns
salt	

Wash the chicken with fresh salt water. Let the meat stand for 1 hour until a lot of grease drips off. Cut off the excess fat, and trim some skin if you wish. (It depends on your taste, whether you want more fat, or less.)

In a large soup pot, put 3 quarts water, salted. Add the meat, allow to boil. Remove the grease and foam that rises to the top. Repeat a few times, until there is almost none.

Add in all the other ingredients. Let it boil on a low heat for at least 60 minutes, until the soup is thick. Remove the meat, cut in small pieces. Place vegetables and meat in a soup dish. Strain the broth. Serve hot with a spoon of fresh grated cheese.

The meat and vegetables can be seasoned with a little more salt and oil and served as a side dish.

3.6.7. Spiedini di vitella (Veal rolls).

This is a very tender and delicate veal rollatini to complete a festive dinner.

Ingredients

2 pounds veal (cut from the leg)	½ pound *prosciutto*
1 cup seasoned bread crumbs	6 cloves finely chopped garlic
½ cup fresh grated *pecorino* cheese	1 spoons finely chopped basil
6 whole bay leaves	1 spoon oregano
½ glass extra virgin olive oil	2 spoons butter

Lay out the meat, one by one on a kitchen counter and cover with brown paper. To tenderize the meat, pound with a heavy kitchen mallet until it is as thin as possible. Take off the paper and cut the meat in pieces of no more than 4 inches.

Mix ½ bread crumbs and the cheese (save the rest of the bread crumbs for coating), and add 2 spoons of extra virgin olive oil. Make a soft mixture.

Place the meat on a large serving dish. On each piece, put a slice of *prosciutto*, a half spoon of the cheese mixture, a few pieces of garlic, a little basil and a pinch of oregano.

Roll the meat. Secure the roll with a toothpick, dip in the oil and coat with the breadcrumbs. Place on a greased baking pan. On each *rollatini* put a pinch of butter and between each put a bay leaf.

Preheat the oven to 350 degrees. Bake for 20 minutes. Serve hot.

Indescribable aroma!!!

3.6.8. Buciullùna (Pork rollers).

This is the most famous dishg for *Martedì Grasso* (Carnival). It is very rich and requires a long time to prepare it, but it is worth it to do it at least once a year. It is cooked deep in a thick tomato sauce, and seasons a dish of *spaghetti*.

Ingredients

6 large boneless pork cutlets	1 pound chopped pork
6 large pieces *prosciutto*	3 hard-boiled eggs, cut in quarters
3 spoons finely chopped basil	6 leaves fresh basil
6 spoons fresh grated *pecorino* cheese	6 garlic cloves, minced
6 spoons butter	salt and pepper

Spaghetti

Ingredients for the sauce

2 cans (28 ounce) peeled tomatoes	1 can 16 ounce tomato paste
3 minced garlic cloves	salt, pepper and *peperoncino* (red hot pepper)

You will need a spool of heavy thread for tying the *braciole* (cutlet).

Place the cutlets on a piece of waxed paper and cover with waxed paper. Pound with a wooden kitchen mallet until the meat is about ¼ inch thick.

Put the cutlets on a large dish. On each, place one large piece of *prosciutto*, 1 spoon chopped meat, 1 spoon cheese, 1 basil leaf, ½ spoon parsley, ¼ spoon butter, little salt, a pinch of black pepper and a pinch of hot pepper.

Roll the cutlets, keeping the mixture inside. Make sure the ends are not open. Cut a piece of thread and tie as much as needed to be sure there are no holes in the meat. Place the *braciole* in a frying pan with oil on all sides. Make sure they do not open.

In a large pot, sauté the garlic, puree the tomatoes and add in. Dilute the tomato paste with double the amount of water and add. Let it boil for 15 minutes. Place the *braciole* in the sauce one by one. Let boil 10 minutes more. Lower the flame and cook for 30 minutes until the sauce is thick.

Cook the spaghetti.

Take the *braciole* out. Take the thread off. With a sharp knife, slice the *braciole* 1 inch wide. Place on a large serving dish. Add 1 spoon of sauce on top.

Pour the rest of the sauce on top of the spaghetti and have the *braciole* for an exotic entrée.

3.6.9. Scaloppine al Marsala (Marsala veal).

The delicious Sicilian Marsala wine can be use like an aperitif or for making a delicious Mediterranean Sicilian salsa to dress this delicate veal dish.

Ingredients

2 pounds veal (cut from the leg)

4 cloves garlic, minced

1 cup Marsala (red sweet wine)

6 spoons butter

4 spoons butter

1 cup flour (for coating the meat)

1 pound mushrooms

Clean the mushrooms, leave whole.

Sauté the garlic, add the mushrooms, sauté for a few minutes, let cook with their own liquid. If needed, add a little water.

Cut the meat in 3 inch square pieces. Salt and coat with the flour on both sides.

Melt the butter in another frying pan, and lightly fry the meat on both sides, sprinkling little by little with the Marsala. Cover and let wine evaporate for 5 minutes. Add the mushrooms. Bring it to a boil. Lower the heat and let cook for 10 minutes more. Serve hot or cold with their own marsala sauce.

VERDURE (VEGETABLES).

In the springtime when all the fresh vegetables like Fave beans, peas, artichokes and shallots are ripe enough to make delicious frittata, we are all anxious to prepare this nutritious and light lunch. We can prepare this aromatic lunch with a small amount of money, and all the family can eat and enjoy a very tasty meal.

Usually, my mother asked me to go with her to the farm to look for the fresh green vegetables. She enjoyed picking them with a small knife and putting them in her pocket. She took everything she saw: all the chicory or other wild herbs growing in the empty spaces.

In the countryside we do not have as many dogs "watering" the crops like in the city. Here the dogs stay at home waiting patiently for the mater to return from work to do his duty. The master, tired from working all day, lets the poor dog stretch his legs instead of taking him for a long walk. At the first empty space he goes, and returns home fast so as not to make his owner wait.

Certainly we cannot pick all the chicory near the city. The really fresh and clean vegetables come directly from the farm, cultivated with care by a person using natural manure, and not chemicals to produce the food we put into our systems. Chemicals ruin the nutritious substances for a more abundant harvest. My *nonna* always had a small garden full of herbs and all kinds of vegetables at the side of the house, ready to be cut by my mother, with the *coltellino* (little knife).

Right now as I write all my memories I feel like I am my mother a long time ago. She used to complain about all the modern technology and artificial chemicals that were harmful to our health. I would listen to her, annoyed and thinking she was so old fashioned not to approve of modern technology.

Now, after so many years…all the stories, advice and recommendations she would tell me…turn to be right. Today I say and repeat things similar to what she used to say. Unfortunately, it is too late to tell her, *Mamma avevi ragione* (Mamma, you were right). Today I want to go to the farm to cut fresh green chicory; nevertheless, under different circumstances I now buy what I can find, making believe I am pleased, and telling myself it is okay.

3.7.1. Frittata con fiori di zucchine (Squash flower frittata).

There are so many styles of frittata in Sicily. Each season produces a different vegetable. Because they are nutritious, it is worth the time to prepare.

This is the most delicate and different from the others. In the summer this squash blooms, and almost every family has zucchini plants. This plant has three different uses: for the zucchini, for the leaves, and for the flowers.

Cut the flower early in the morning when they are in full bloom. Cut the seed inside. Gently wash and dry.

Ingredients

12 flowers

2 beaten eggs

2 finely minced garlic cloves

½ cup bread crumbs

½ cup grated cheese

½ cup bisquick

salt

2 spoons butter, for frying

Mix the eggs, cheese, bread crumbs, salt. Dip the flowers gently in the mix, and try to keep the flowers open.

Melt the butter with 2 spoons oil and fry the flower on both sides for a few minutes. Dry. Serve immediately.

3.7.2. Frittata di asparagi (Asparagus frittata).

In the springtime, in the mountains under the rocks after a heavy rain, the wild asparagus started to appear all over. The brownish green colored stalk was tall and shiny, full of bloom, and spiny. They have a different taste, and are very good.

Ingredients

1 pound asparagus

6 beaten eggs

1 spoons fresh grated cheese

2 spoons bread crumbs

salt and pepper

Wash the asparagus. Cut off the hard end.

Put a glass of water into a fry pan and add the asparagus. Let boil for 8 to 10 minutes. Drain the water. Add oil, and let fry on both sides a few minutes.

Mix the eggs, cheese, bread crumbs, and salt and pour on the asparagus. Sprinkle the cheese on the top. Cover and let cook until the liquid is absorbed. Take off the cover.

Take a dish a little larger than the frying pan and put it upside down on the pan. Turn the fry pan over onto the dish so that the frittata drops into the dish. Add a little more oil to the fry pan if needed, and return the frittata to the fry pan to cook the other side. Let fry a few more minutes. Remove and serve hot.

If you don't want to fry the frittata, after boiling, place the frittata into an oiled baking pan and add the mixture and sprinkle on the cheese. Fry for a few minutes or bake in the oven.

3.7.3. *Carciofi fritti* (Fried hartichokes).

The most tasty artichokes are the smallest. They are more tender and have less (hair) in the middle. Sicily is the best place for the cultivation of artichokes. The sun, the temperature, and the ground are the perfect combination for the plant to grow and mature. It gives the artichoke a superb taste. After eating them, drink a glass of water, and a pleasant anisette taste will tickle your palate.

Ingredients

6 artichokes

2 beaten eggs

1 cup flour

2 spoons fresh grated cheese

2 garlic cloves

1 spoon yeast

Juice of ½ lemon (for the wash water)

Mix the eggs, yeast, flour and cheese. Let rest.

Cut the spine from the artichokes.
Wash the artichokes in water with a few drops of lemon to keep them from turning dark. Take off the side hard leaves, leave the tender middle heart.
Take off the middle hair.
Cut them in the middle, in a few slices.

In a frying pan, heat the oil. Dip each artichoke piece in the mixture. Pick them up in a spoon to keep more of the mixture on the artichoke. Place in the pan and fry for a few minutes, until golden. Place them on paper towel to remove excess oil. Serve warm or cold, for a picnic day.

3.7.4. *Cardi fritti.*

This is the artichoke's hard stem. Take off all the spine, the hard side, the velvet cover. Cut the tender part in 4 inch pieces. Boil 10 minutes.

Dry. Dip in the same mixture as the artichokes. Fry for a few minutes. They are delicious.

3.7.5. *Carciofi ripieni* (Stuffed artichokes).

After a long, magnificent dinner, for the finish and to help digestion, it is tradition to end with these artichokes. After they are cooked, make sure you keep them in a place where they can be seen, because sometimes we forget this good vegetable. Serve with the meal as a side dish.

Ingredients

6 artichokes

3 spoons grated fresh cheese

3 spoons bread crumbs

6 spoons basil, finely chopped

6 cloves minced garlic

12 spoons extra virgin olive oil

salt, and lots of pepper

Juice of one lemon (for wash water)

Cut the spine. Take off all of the round hard petals. Wash the artichokes with fresh water and the lemon juice. Take the stem off the artichoke so it will sit securely and push down to try to open the petals to better stuff them. Mix all the ingredients together with salt and pepper. Add in 6 spoons oil. Leave the other six for seasoning at the end. Divide the mixture in 6 parts.

Distribute the mixture on top of each petal. Repeat until all are stuffed.

Put 2 glasses of water in a deep pot. Place the artichokes in the pot one at a time.

Put one spoon of oil in the middle of each one. Bring to a boil and lower the heat. Cover and let them cook for 15–20 minutes until the petals are all tender.

To test to see if they are done, try to pull off a petal. If it comes off easily, it is done.

3.7.6. *Caponatina* (Eggplant).

This dish is extremely Sicilian, with wild ingredients from our mountain, like capers and oregano with really exotic taste.

Ingredients

2 eggplant, cut in pieces

½ cup green olives (pitted and chopped)

1 can tomato puree (28 ounce)

1 stick celery, cut in pieces

½ cup capers (wash)

½ glass red vinegar

3 spoons sugar

1 spoon oregano

4 leaves basil

2 garlic cloves (finely minced)

Wash the eggplant and soak in salt water for a few minutes. Dry, and fry in hot oil. Drain off the oil. Boil the celery for 15 minutes until soft, add the olives and the capers. Let boil 5 minutes. Drain and set aside.

Sauté the garlic and prepare a thick tomato sauce, cook for 10 minutes. Add the eggplant and the other ingredients. Mix the vinegar with the sugar and add to the sauce. Add a pinch of oregano, salt and pepper. Cook on high heat for a few minutes. Lower the heat and cook 10 minutes more. Cool and serve.

Good for antipasto or lunch. Will keep in refrigerator for a long time.

3.7.7. *Insalata di pomodoro e cipolla* (Tomato and onion salad).

This is the most traditional familiar salad. Easy, economical, healthy.

Ingredients

4 green tomatoes

2 green cucumbers

1 red onion

1 spoon oregano

¼ cup extra virgin olive oil

4 fresh basil leaves

2 spoons red wine vinegar

salt and pepper

Dice all the ingredients. Season with oil, vinegar, salt and pepper. Mix, eat, in good health.

3.7.8. *Insalata di arance e finocchi* (Orange and fennel salad).

In January when the frigid temperature freezes the other fruits, the orange is ripe, with their own perfume aroma. The farm smells so good, you will want to harvest with your hands from tie tree.

This salad is so simple and good.

Ingredients

2 mature oranges

1 fennel

¼ cut balsamic vinegar

¼ cut extra virgin olive oil (from Sicily_

½ spoon fresh oregano

salt, pepper

Cut the orange in small pieces
Cut the fennel in small pieces
Season with the vinegar, salt, pepper and sprinkle with fresh oregano.
Prepare and let rest to be more tasty.

3.7.9. *Insalata di lattuga romana* (Roman lettuce salad).

Use the fresh, tender leaves for this refreshing salad.

1 bunch lettuce

Juice of three lemons

3 oiled anchovies

1 glass extra virgin olive oil

Cut the lettuce, add the lemon juice, the sardines and the oil. Season with lots of pepper and salt to taste. (Anchovies are very salty.)

3.7.10. *Insalata di spinaci* (spinaci salad).

Years ago we only ate spinach cooked. Little by little we have discovered that it is very nutritious and can be eaten raw in a salad. It is wonderful.

Today it is one of the best tasting salads and is used frequently for any occasion.

Ingredients

½ pound fresh spinach leaves

2 spoons pignoli (pine nuts)

2 spoons raisins

4 tangerines

2 spoons parmesan, cut in pieces

½ cup balsamic vinegar

½ cup extra virgin olive oil

¼ spoon fresh oregano

Salt, pepper

Wash the spinach leaves in fresh water, making sure to remove all the sand.
Peel the tangerines and cut in small pieces. Remove any seeds.
Cut the pignoli in half. Add the other ingredients.
Dress with the oil, vinegar, salt and pepper.
It is so good for the palate, and healthier for the stomach. Enjoy.

3.7.11. *Castagne arrostite* (roasted chestnuts).

In winter time, even on the coldest nights, we would take a passeggiata (stroll). Yes, a Sunday passeggiata, even in the winter.

First of all, the winter was not so very frigid, even so, we put on our coats, scarves and gloves and got ready to go to lu chianu. The piazza was entertainment for us in every season. It sounds incredible, but even when the sky looked dark and looked like it might rain, instead of staying home we would still go and bring an umbrella. If the rain was really a storm, we would return home reluctantly. This almost never happened. It rarely rains in Sicily, and we hoped it never would on Sunday. After a few hours of strolling up and down, down and up, we would return home tired and hungry.

Only on the way back we could buy some food. We were prohibited by my parents to eat on the way out because if we ate then we would get our clothes and faces dirty and look sloppy. So we had to wait.

Walking home we met the street vendors that still were there with their small carts in the middle of the street, near the small charcoal fire furnace, waiting to sell the roasted chestnuts.

Before roasting, they would make a little cut in the center of the chestnut so they wouldn't explode. They would sprinkle them with lots of salt. In a few minutes, the shell became brownish gray. The hard chestnuts became soft, taste good, and you can smell the aroma from a few blocks away. If you did not know where they were situated, you could follow the smoke. Before you reached them, your mouth would be watering. When you got there, a few people would be all around the fire, to buy the chestnuts, talking and getting warm.

For 25 or 30 lire they would give you 10 or 15 chestnuts, spooned into a newspaper cone that they had quickly made out of ready cut square pieces of old newspaper. We were never happy with the amount we received. We always argued for a few more. The vendor would complain that the chestnut season that year was poor, but in the meantime, he would give a few more to leave the customer happy.

You see, in Sicily, even if you buy a small amount of something they spend more time to argue than to buy, because they have so much free time.

The customers complain all the time.

The price they first ask is double high.

The buyer complains.

The vendor starts to justify his high expenses.

Finally, when we both are happy, we return home, eating the hot roasted chestnuts that warm the mouth and the body. That simple food lingers on my palate still today.

Another food sold on the street in winter was the boiled "carciofini", the small artichokes. They were the smallest; none bigger than a couple of inches. They were boiled in salt water, drained, and a few were put into the cones, usually newspaper. There was no plastic for us at that time. Before we reached home, we would scrape each piece through our teeth and throw the empty petal on the street. At that time were not thinking about keeping the street clean. We thought that was the garbage man's job to clean it the next day. We enjoyed eating, walking, talking. Maybe we didn't even know what we did was wrong. Today is another life still. It is sad to hear that the men that do it are too old, or die.

Now the "Pizzeria" is the substitute for the street carts. The young prefer something else. The modern world replaces the street vendor with its expensive restaurants, and the coffee shops, and the young people don't know the fun they miss.

Or maybe we miss the fun they have. I think every generation has their own fun ways to enjoy, but it is hard for the old to understand!

Sicilia giardino d'Europa (Sicily, Europe's garden).

There is no better place for growing food than Sicily with its fertile ground, the bright sun and the mild winter temperatures. It is the perfect climate for sun-ripened fruits and vegetables.

As the proverb says: "Ogni frutto a suo tempo." Every fruit ripens in its own season."

Today, everything is canned. With modern cultivation we have everything in all seasons. We need to have the patience to wait for the right time for fruit to become really tasty.

THE FRUITS

Almost all year round, the farms have something to cultivate. They start in January with the orange, that special *tarocchi*, or *sanguinelli*. The lemon, in full blossom with their own white flower Zagara. They perfumed the air with a really Sicilian odor from *Mediterraneo*.

The lemon, the tangerine, the *nespole* (a little orange oval fruit, full of big seeds, but very tasty). The *zorbe,* another exotic fruit; round and brown. They are cut very green and kept in a dark place for a few weeks to ripen, and become a dark, soft, sweet fruit. The prickly pear, with the pungent spine. When it is ripe it has to be cut in a special way to not be hurt. What a taste!

The mirtillo, white and black, is very small, like a very small cherry shape with a lot of little seeds. Some become ripe in their own season (with patience), and became another exotic fruit to enjoy together with more ordinary fruits like *fragole* (strawberry), *finocchi, gelsi* (white and black), *mele* (apple), *fichi* (black and white) etc.

THE CHEESE

Another Sicilian specialty is fresh cheese. There are so many varieties, like the famous *caciocavallo* (horse cheese) from Ragusa, the *pecorino* (from the lamb), the fresh *tuma* (from the goat). The most tasty for me is the fresh *pepato* cheese with the whole pepper. This is the tasty and famous cheese exported from Sciacca all over the world.

THE COLD MEATS

In the winter time when the pork is butchered, the meat and the lard are salted and put in the special animal intestines and dried for a few months. After they have dried well they become the best *salami, morta-della, subbissata,* and *prosciutto*. My favorite is the dry sausages. Years ago, my father home made the pork sausages and hung them up on a bamboo cane that was in the high ceiling. Before it was good and dry we would have some pieces with home-made bread for lunch or supper at night.

THE SALT

The salt is our white gold. The famous *saline* in Trapani, that natural marine salt, became one of the most natural seasonings after drying on the sandy beach (with no salt, I think nothing is so tasty or healthy).

THE OLIVE OIL

The olives on the magnificent century olive tree with strong tall branches would be almost ripe in November, and ready for the first harvest. The first harvest is for the big still hard green olives. Some of the harvest, after a salting procedure, became *olive salate* (salted olives).

Buy a few pounds of fresh green olives. One at a time, cover the olive with a paper towel and crush the olive with a wooden kitchen mallet. Let them open a little. Leave the pit inside.

Keep in fresh water for 5 days, changing the water each day until they are less bitter. Prepare plenty of salt (marine salt, if possible). The old way was to put enough water to cover the olives in a glass or ceramic container and put in one raw egg. Start to add salt. When the egg starts to go to the top of the water, there is enough salt. Remove the egg. Dissolve the salt well (if possible, prepare the salt water a few days ahead of time). Add a few whole garlic cloves, a branch of fresh oregano and add the crushed olives. Cover them. In a week, with a large slotted kitchen spoon, you can take out the olives you want to eat. Rinse and season with extra virgin oil, a pinch of fresh oregano, a little minced garlic and a sprinkle of vinegar. Have a piece of semolina bread ready for dipping. *Buon appetito*!!! A very tasty delicacy.

Another delicacy is the dry black olives. For this, wait until the olives are mature, and oily. After a few weeks of sun drying, salting and curing every day, with time and patience, they became another gourmet food.

ThePassuluna (sun dry, salted olives)

In a wicker basket put the black olives and salt them. Let them stay in the sun and stir frequently until the liquid drips out. Repeat salting and stirring in the sun for a few days until they are very dry.

Prepare a container and place the dry olives inside. Cover with olive oil. Add a few fresh basil leaves. This can stay for a long time. Eat the olives seasoned with fresh extra virgin oil and a pinch of oregano. They can be added to salads, eaten plain, or fried.

This is a lot of work. Years ago, the time for the woman did not matter, so they used their time working in the kitchen, and it was worth it to make these with a really natural Sicilian taste.

Estratto di pomodoro (Tomato paste)

The sun ripens the tomato and it is ready for harvest, the farms are so colorful with beautiful reds. The farmers after a long laborious work day are satisfied that the crop is ripe and ready to pick, harvesting more and more everyday. My grandfather saved the seeds from the year before; they are dried from the sun and are ready the following year. After he prepared the soil he planted the different types of seeds. Some of the tomatoes are pear shaped; others were big and round and suitable for making salads with red onion, cucumbers and oil, salt, pepper and oregano, generously obtained from the mountains. Or peeled and squeezed into jars, removing the seeds and sprinkling a pinch of salt and putting basil leaves that have been boiled in a *bagno Maria* (double sauce pan) for a few minutes to use for making *pizza* sauce in the winter.

Another way was to cut them in the middle and squeeze the juice, putting salt on each piece situated in *cannistri* (Bamboo basket). Exposed to the hot sun for a few days, and every night bought them inside the house and then the next day put them in the sun again until they got dried. The taste is so good and there are so many uses of them.

Little cherry tomatoes were the most important for us. When they were fully ripened the men started to put them one by one in a large basket called *panàru*. After filling the basket they would bring it inside to a cool place. Early in the morning when some were ready, my mother would start to wash them and put them in the sun to dry and one by one take off the steam...my sister and I would help with this. We would cut them in the middle, throw them in a big pot and let all the water drip out, leaving only the thick pulp.

My mother was ready for *passarli a setaccio* (sieving). She put the sieve on top of the table and screwed the bottom platform tight in a corner leaving the side open with the juice exiting freely going into the pot. With a wood spatula, she would squeeze all the tomato collecting the thick red juice in a large ceramic pot. The seeds would be placed in a different dish ready to be exposed to the sun, dried for the next year's seeding (basically recycling).

Before the sieving was finished, we prepared a few big flat wooden tables, standing at an angle (to let the liquid drip off). We put the thick juice in top of the table add a few spoons of sea salt and let it stay in the hot sun all day. With a wood spoon, we would turn it repeatedly and watch the flies going around, but make sure they did not land!!! In the meantime the juice would start to get thicker. At sunset the dried tomato in the pot is about to be ready for the next day. With love and patience my dear mother returns the almost dried liquid from the table, and despite the hot sun it needs to be dried more. Finally after a few days and a little more drying, the juice becoming less and less from the pot until it is a very thick and dark red paste, smelling so good. It was placed in a very hot glass jar (uncovered in the sun with a spoon of olive oil and basil leaves on top). It was covered very tightly and conserved in a cool place, remaining for a long time, smelling so fresh and ready to be used in the wintertime. It is the perfect dressing for a good dish of spaghetti!!!

Summary

About the Author

Maria Marchese Sciortino was born in Sciacca, Sicily, Italy in 1938. Three months after her marriage to her childhood sweetheart, Alphonso in 1961, she immigrated to Brooklyn, New York where she raised her two sons and worked as a dressmaker. 44 years later, Maria has 6 grandchildren and enjoys writing about her life in modern America and old world Italy. She is now retired and divides her time between her home in Staten Island and Naples, Florida.

978-0-595-37552-3
0-595-37552-9

Printed in the United Kingdom by
Lightning Source UK Ltd., Milton Keynes
139104UK00002B/147/A